The Dictionary of
Fashionable Nonsense

The Dictionary of Fashionable Nonsense

A Guide for Edgy People

By Ophelia Benson
and Jeremy Stangroom

SOUVENIR PRESS

First published in Great Britain in 2004 by Souvenir Press
43 Great Russell Street, London WC1B 3PD

ISBN 0 285 63714 2

Typeset by FiSH Books, London
Printed and bound in Great Britain by Creative Print and Design
Group (Wales), Ebbw Vale

Acknowledgements

It is, of course, very fashionable to name-drop, or rather, to thank people at the beginning of a book. So here are the people we want to thank. Ernest Hecht and his team at *Souvenir* for all their help in putting this book together. Elfreda Powell for exemplary editing skills. Katinka Matson and Russell Weinberger for helping to frame the original proposal for the book. Steve Pinker for his kind help and for finding the book funny. John Lipczynksi for thanking one of the authors of this book in his latest book. And Bill Gates, Britney Spears and the Dalai Lama for being very famous. Also, they are, of course, very inspirational – well, two of them are, at any rate. It goes without saying that none of these people is responsible for any of the shortcomings of this book. These are, in fact, down to James Forrester of 21 Artichoke Way, Bristol.

Introduction

The world, of course, is full of fashionable nonsense. Feng Shui, pilates, Naomi Campbell, Pop Idol, Manolo Blahnik footwear, the list is endless. However, this dictionary is concerned with one particular species of fashionable nonsense, the kind found in certain unswept corners of academe.

No doubt the idea that there are fashionable corners of the academy *at all* will strike many people as being unlikely. And it is true that we're not talking here about fashion in the sense of wearing trendy clothes or dining at hip restaurants. We're talking rather about a certain way of seeing the world, one which enables us to decide all questions in our own favour, to ignore countervailing evidence, to draw just those conclusions which we want. This is clearly such a useful thing that it is not surprising that it is fashionable. But how is it done? What's the trick?

Easy. Just claim that truth is in the eye of the beholder. That we all have our own versions of the truth and that no one of them actually corresponds to the way things really are in the world. Once you swallow this particular conceit, then pretty much anything goes. Want to claim that the lost city of Atlantis is at the bottom of your neighbour's garden? No problem, just reject any demand that you should supply some evidence for your belief as an infringement of your right to your own culture. Are you a devotee of homeopathic remedies? You're in luck. You can dismiss the mass of evidence showing that homeopathy has no effect with a cheery wave and a discourse on the hegemonic encroachment of Western medical techniques. What's best of all is that you don't even need to understand what this means.

Surely this sort of thing doesn't go on in the universities and colleges of higher education? At least, not in the good ones? Well, you'd be surprised. This kind of nonsense is established in a great many, though not all, parts of academe. No department of humanities is entirely – or, perhaps, even a little – free of it, and among the social sciences perhaps only the more empirical branches of economics, sociology and psychology keep their hems out of the mud. Here are some examples.

Anthropologist Frederique Apffel Marglin wants to 'challenge science's claim to be a superior form of knowledge which renders obsolete more traditional systems of thought.' But she is confronted by the fact that Western medicine has eradicated smallpox from the world. No problem. She performs a tidy back-flip, and tells us that 'in absolutely negativizing disease, suffering and death…the scientific medical system of knowledge…can and does objectify people with all the repressive political possibilities that objectification opens.' You'd do well to remember this the next time you visit your doctor with a fever.

Or how about the writers of Theory – Literary Theory, Cultural Theory, Critical Theory, and the most prestigious of all, just plain Theory – who lean on clotted jargon and tortured syntax to make no point at all. When criticised for writing in such a pompous and unreadable style, they defend their practice by saying that it is the only way to 'perform' the unreliability of language. What's more, they'll tell you, it is precisely this unreliability which means that nobody can say quite what they mean to say. For people who aren't saying much at all, this is probably very convenient.

And then there are the anti-Darwinians. It is fair to say that most people in academe broadly accept Darwinian theory so long as its insights are used *only* to explain the behaviour of non-human animals. But anybody who dares to suggest that Darwinism might have some applicability for understanding human beings is in for a rough ride from a faction of Leftist academics. More than likely they'll be accused of reductionism, social Darwinism, imperialism, genetic determinism, eugenicism, sexism, racism and a whole gamut of other isms. And if they're very lucky, then, like Ed Wilson, author of the groundbreaking *Sociobiology*, they'll also have a pitcher of water tipped over their head.

These examples are barely even the tip of the iceberg as far as academic nonsense goes. There are also the delights of psycho-analysis, deconstructionism, ecofeminism, Afrocentric history, critical legal studies, the sociology of knowledge, difference feminism, and so on. And you'll notice that *The Dictionary of Fashionable Nonsense* covers all this stuff, and a lot more besides. However, you might be puzzled by its inclusion of a number of scientific terms. Surely scientists are made of sterner stuff than they need to bend the truth to their own whims and fancies?

Well, indeed they are. Science in academe is almost entirely free of this kind of wilful truth denying, reality bending and wishful thinking. However, a whole branch of fashionable nonsense amuses itself by pinching the ideas and vocabulary of the sciences. Presumably the hope is that it will somehow boost its credibility by its association with the discipline it so often despises. So what you find is that portentous mentions of quantum gravity and quantum other things, of chaos and complexity, fractals and butterflies, quarks and attractors, and that dear old stand-by relativity, turn up in many a critical theory and cultural studies musing. Of course, almost inevitably these quasi-scientific ruminations are founded on concepts misunderstood and misapplied. But this doesn't stop anybody: silly things go on being said and hollow mentions of chaos and quantumness go on being made, so into the dictionary they go.

Why does all this matter? Why does it warrant being satirised in a dictionary of this kind? It matters because truth matters. If we understand how the world works, then we can make people's lives better. We can feed them by making use of GM technology to increase crop yields. We can keep them healthy by developing new kinds of antibiotics, better vaccines and more powerful treatments for illnesses such as cancer and AIDS. And can keep them safe by making *well-founded* risk assessments of various environmental threats, such as global warming and the erosion of biodiversity.

And it also matters because if human intelligence matters, if clear thinking and reason and open eyes are good things, then fashionable nonsense really is important and worth resisting. *The*

Dictionary of Fashionable Nonsense is our contribution to this fight against the erosion of reason.

The Dictionary

Reading Key: Words in SMALL CAPS are cross-references.

Absolute Zero
Since there are no absolutes it might seem unlikely that there is such a thing. But absolute zero is not zero at all. It's –273° centigrade, which is less than zero, which just goes to show that zero isn't absolute. It's worth pointing out that things move very slowly at this kind of temperature, so if you're planning a journey and it's this cold, allow more time.

Acceptance
Nice, warm, cooperative way of evaluating ideas, much better than argument.

Accommodate
What to do with criticisms of your favourite ideas if you can't reject them.

Accuracy
Exploded concept. Foolish, Platonic notion that we can get our facts straight.

Acupuncture

A good excuse to stick needles in people you don't like. The blunter the better.

Ad hoc

How to set up your theories so that they can accommodate whatever new evidence comes along, including of course evidence that might seem flatly to disprove your original hypothesis.

Adaptation

What you have to be good at to survive as an academic. The people on your tenure committee are mad for FOUCAULT? You decide now is not the time to publish that coldly lucid deconstruction of the French polymath. The hiring committee at infinitely desirable urban edgy Paradise University are arch-Deleuzo-Guattarians? You take some fast lessons in pretending to understand what they mean. Thus your offspring will survive to grow up and get jobs selling insurance.

Adaptive radiation

A concept denoting the evolution of a variety of species from a single evolutionary stock. The idea is that you take say a Galapagos finch, blast it with gamma rays, and then you get a turkey, which is very useful at Christmas time. Unfortunately, evolution is unpredictable, so you might get a dung beetle, which wouldn't be quite so good. Large experiments in adaptive radiation have been conducted in recent times at Three Mile Island and Chernobyl. These turned out to be a bit dodgy, which just goes to show how ill-advised are the current GM CROPS trials in the UK.

Admiration

The currency of academic life.

Adorno, Theodore

Member of the Frankfurt School. Co-wrote the influential *Dialectic of Enlightenment* with Max Horkheimer. Friend of the much hipper Walter Benjamin. All wrong about jazz and the culture industry. Either too Marxist or not Marxist enough.

Agoric drive

Psychic pressure to go shopping. Doesn't apply so much to trips to the supermarket, which are thought to be linked more to the famic or mangic drive, but rather to shopping for clothes, shoes, kitchen toys, electronic objects, ornaments. See SCOPIC DRIVE.

Alienation

Primarily a Marxist idea denoting the separation of man from the fruits of his labour and ultimately from his SPECIES BEING. So what does this mean? Well, supposing you work in a factory making biros. You make twenty a day. Do you take twenty biros home with you every day? No, you don't. And that's a bad thing. Because you've invested part of your being, if you like, in those biros. Part of what it is to be human is to make things like biros in concert with other human beings. So you're alienated. You would think that this would be a bad thing, but oddly enough people don't seem to mind too much. Mind you, MARX anticipated this – he argued that capitalism provides material compensation for alienation. But this can't go on for ever. Although it does seem to be going on a bit longer than anticipated. Nevertheless revolution is just around the corner, we're simply in an age of waiting at the moment. See AS OPPOSED TO WHAT, PROLETARIAT.

Alphabet

The opposite of the Goddess. Leonard Shlain puts it this way in *The Goddess and the Alphabet*: 'But one pernicious effect of literacy has gone largely unnoticed: writing subliminally fosters a patriarchal outlook. Writing of any kind, but especially its alphabetic form, diminishes feminine values and with them, women's power in the culture.'

Alternative
A wonderful thing. Because it's the opposite of everything. You have the regular, normal, boring thing, like MEDICINE, or scholarship, or EDUCATION, and then you have the alternative kind, which does whatever the opposite is. Normal medicine relies on testing, so alternative medicine relies on guesswork and hunches and an inner voice. So much more SPIRITUAL.

Alternative medicine
Feisty cousin of complementary medicine. Tends to dress in black and likes droning rock music. Although it includes things like HOMEOPATHY and psychic surgery, there's no truth to the rumour that people seeking out alternative treatments would be better off seeing a psychiatrist. See CHARLES, COMPLEMENTARY MEDICINE, MEDICINE.

Althusser, Louis
French, structural Marxist, more famous for strangling his wife whilst giving her neck a massage than for his theories, but important for introducing expressions like interpellation and ideological state apparatus into uncommon parlance.

Always already
Profound, resonant phrase used in Theory to convey (without actually coming right out and saying it) that theorists know everything and always have. Everything was always already going to be or do whatever it is the theorist is talking about, which somehow leaves the impression that the theorist made it happen.

Ambiguity

1) Something that William Empson discovered there were seven kinds of – though now that Theory has come along, it could probably find a lot more than that if it tried.

2) A very useful tool for theoretical DISCOURSE because it means there is never any need to say anything precise or specific or clear; there is no need to define one's terms or justify one's arguments (much less have anything to do with logic), one can just string words together and, if naive people either disagree or say it's unclear, one just talks about ambiguity and indeterminacy and that's the end of that.

Ancestor

The problem with ancestors is that there isn't normally much left of them. Just a few bones, if you're lucky. This means that bones must always be treated with respect. For example, you can't just bring your dog along to an archaeological dig in the hope that she'll strike it lucky. Nor can you allow SCIENTISTS to go around haphazardly pinching bits of bodies. Basically, the bones of ancestors should not be stuck in museums, nor should they appear on the mantelpieces of scientists, especially if they have been claimed by indigenous people. See ARCHAEOLOGY.

Anguish

Has a technical meaning and an everyday meaning. Its technical meaning has to do with freedom. Imagine that you're on the top of a cliff. You are clutching your latest experimental text. Your beret is twitching in the wind. Do you give up your text to the elements? Allow it to float on the winds of meaning ever-delayed? Or do you stick it in your briefcase and catch the next bus home? Anguish lies in the awareness that any decision you make is not enough; that there is no guarantee that at the next moment you will not change your mind. So your text remains ephemeral, forever in doubt. In its everyday sense, anguish just means feeling a bit pissed off. See SARTRE.

Anomie

The term can refer to the experience of social ALIENATION, but in sociology it doesn't. However, people – well, undergraduates mainly – never remember this, so it represents an excellent opportunity to lord it over them. What does it mean? In its Durkheimian sense, it refers to the breakdown of the social norms which govern society's smooth functioning. This is a bad thing. It is associated with suicide, for example, which itself is bad, unless it involves some tragic literary figure (see CHATTERTON). And it can result in people running around naked, taking a dead chicken home to meet their parents, or even falling asleep during a lecture on DERRIDA. Though perhaps this last example is a little too far-fetched to be taken seriously. See DURKHEIM.

Anthropology

Mainly an excuse for trips to exotic destinations and for patronising indigenous people. Anthropology was a very bad thing a hundred years ago. Nude people studied by lewd people, as some wag once put it. Happily things have improved a bit since then. You'll even find anthropologists who are advocates of NATIVE RIGHTS MOVEMENTS. And who recognise that truth is relative to cultures, well the cultures of indigenous people at least. But still, anthropology is mainly about the trips. After all, how many anthropologists do you find studying the indigenous people of Siberia? Not as many as you'll find studying native Tuscans, I'll bet.

Anticipate

Verb to use when referring to work that precedes and influenced work of admired follower, who is hipper because of being born later. So, for instance, the work of Guy Debord 'anticipates' that of Baudrillard – it was Baudrillard who thought of it, and this Debord fella who wrote about it first somehow clairvoyantly saw ahead and correctly figured out what he was going to say. It's remarkable how many people 'anticipated' the work of theorists and postmodernists.

Anything goes

Technical phrase in the philosophy of science coined by Paul FEYERABEND. Means, roughly, it's too much trouble to explain deduction and induction so figure them out for yourself.

Appeal to authority

If noisy neighbours move in next to your holiday home in TUSCANY, you have the option of appealing to the local Italian authorities in order to get them evicted. A similar kind of tactic can be employed to deal with uppity interlocutors in the academic world. For example, suppose some precocious undergraduate objects to your latest TRANSGRESSIVE theory. You simply ask her what her view is of Deleuze's response to that particular objection. This works pretty much every time because very few people have actually read any Deleuze. If it turns out that your uppity undergraduate is the one person in the whole world to have read all Deleuze's works, your best bet is to bribe her with an offer of a free holiday in Tuscany.

Arbitrary plural

It's very hip and knowing to add random 's's to abstract words that don't normally have them: literatures, knowledges, futures, etc. This undermines the totalising essentialism and reductionist universalisation of modernism, and reveals how multiple, fragmented, FISSURED and hard to count everything is. There is no knowledge, there are knowledges; no literature, only literatures. This of course has the additional advantage of creating the potential for ever more new university departments.

Archaeologist

Nasty kind of SCIENTIST who steals the remains of indigenous people's parents and grandparents, and takes them off to play with in pointless buildings called 'museums'. Archaeologists try to justify this behaviour by saying the remains are thousands of years old and therefore unlikely to be the ancestors of the people who live there

11

now, but that's false, an ancestor is an ancestor, no matter how many generations there are in between. People then say at that rate amoeba, algae and single-celled organisms were our ancestors too, and we could all be walking on or breathing in our ancestors at any moment so we'd better just kill ourselves and join them before we commit any more disrespectful acts. But of course amoeba aren't indigenous people's ancestors because that's not what their grandparents told them and their grandparents told them about how they got here, and archaeologists are very disrespectful and EUROCENTRIC and bad to say their creation stories are truer than anyone else's. Besides archaeologists are strangely preoccupied with the past and dead people, we ought to pay attention to the living and forget all about the dead and the past, because who cares.

Argument
Unpleasant, testosterone-driven method of supporting one's assertions, to be avoided in favour of acceptance.

Aristotle
A famous thief. Stole all his ideas from the library at Alexandria, built after his death, which just goes to show how sneaky he was. See PLATO, SOCRATES.

Armchair
All-purpose adjective meaning: lazy, unhealthy, indoor, cowardly ('armchair general'), bookish, abstract, arbitrary, invented, and different from what I think, as in 'armchair philosopher,' 'armchair anthropologist,' etc.

Art
1) The opposite of science. Akin to religion but with prettier clothes. Special, creative, spiritual, about beauty and harmony. Includes painting, music, folk art (baskets, embroidery, sandals, CROP CIRCLES), sculpture, and possibly literature

although that's tricky because literature is quite domineering and tyrannical, because it's in language and language often pretends to mean something specific.

2) An empty category. A distinction without a difference. An example of the narcissism of small differences. Everything is art, or else nothing is. If a painting is, so is a footprint. If music is, so is yelling. If sculpture is, so is a bucket of sand. If literature is, so is a telephone book. The artificial HIERARCHY of what's art and what is just ordinary is what keeps us all in chains.

As opposed to what

Rude, offensive question often asked by sceptics. When theorists are saying profound things about alienation, or HOSPITALS as curing machines, or the negativisation of illness and death, there is often a scientistic or positivist type in the area who will say in an unpleasant tone, 'As opposed to what?' A spot of LOCOMOTION WITHOUT A GOAL can come in handy at such times.

Assertion

1) Essential technique, replacing the need for argument and evidence.

2) To be greeted with acceptance, rather than argument.

Assimilation

What powerful cultures do to less powerful cultures. Like the Borg from *Star Trek*. The whole earth under threat from an alien race which models itself on a Swedish tennis player. Scary stuff. Anyway, just like the way the Borg assimilate whole planets, so powerful cultures assimilate whole other cultures. This is bad, even if the assimilated claim that it is not. Which, irritatingly, they frequently do. They just don't know their place these days.

Assumption

Something to be examined when it is our opponent's and taken for granted when it is our own.

Astrology

Not really scientific, apparently, but there seems to be too much in it just to dismiss completely. A compromise seems like the best solution. It's not 100 percent true but it's maybe 15 percent, 10 percent, something like that. It's not very true, but it's a little bit true.

Astronomy

The result of a collaboration by Copernicus and Galileo, astronomy is the science of constellations. The most exciting thing about astronomy is that it enables a person to look back in time using a telescope. If you take a peek at the sun, for example – telescope not required – you're watching something that happened eight minutes ago. This kind of visual time-travel does have practical benefits. For example, if you're about to die, then likely you will be comforted by the thought that your friends on Alpha Centauri will have the pleasure of your company, admittedly at a distance, for another four years. Astronomers are interested in things other than time-travel. They like building things – mainly telescopes, it must be said – on tops of mountains. This is so they can get slightly nearer to the stars. Proximity brings advantages. Halley's comet, when it can be bothered to turn up, is transformed from a pinprick into a smudge. But strangely the sun doesn't appear to be much bigger when you're up a mountain. Probably a trick of the light. See FAIRIES AT THE BOTTOM OF THE GARDEN.

Atomism

An Ancient Greek idea – probably the start of all our problems. Leucippus and Democritus suggested that the world could be broken down into indivisible particles. If this were true – which it isn't – it would just have been a lucky guess. Unfortunately, even though it isn't true, lots of people have proceeded as if it were true, which has resulted in REDUCTIONISM and linear reasoning. So the Greeks have a lot to answer for. See HOLISM, OLYMPIC GAMES.

Attitude

The basic building block of any decent EPISTEMOLOGY. Get the attitude right and the rest will fall into place. The right attitude includes but is not limited to: unconditional love, tolerance, inclusiveness, appreciation of diversity, acceptance of difference, loyalty, sensitivity, empathy. Get these right and you'll avoid most of the worst mistakes scholars and inquirers can make, such as failing to admire, or even actually criticising, other people's institutions, religions, customs, political arrangements, caste systems, or ways of knowing.

Attitude adjustment

New way of doing politics. Huge improvement on old way, because so much less work. No need to reform institutions or laws; instead simply change everyone's attitudes to institutions and laws, and the effect is exactly the same. So with FEMINISM, for example, simply persuade everyone that being warm and nurturing and intuitive is better than being clever and independent, and everyone's happy. If that sounds exactly like the bad old days when women were nonentities and lived lives of total frustration and balked potential – it's not, it's completely different, because this new view of women is much more sophisticated, and backed up by really clever French philosophy.

Audience

Along with innovation, risk and FISSURE, the audience is the lifeblood of the academic world. If a Theorist has spent a couple of hours writing her latest TRANSGRESSIVE text, she isn't going to be too happy if there is nobody to share it with. She needs an audience.

The trouble is the only people who are interested in transgressive texts are other people who write transgressive texts. So what has emerged is a situation where Theorists take it in turn to be the audience for other Theorists. It's a kind of you rub my text, I'll rub yours situation. Without any actual rubbing, obviously. That would be weird.

Author
Imaginary being; artificial abstract category that doesn't really exist. Western capitalist individualistic word to explain how texts are produced. The idea is that one person 'writes' a text, and that person is the author. Obvious what a EUROCENTRIC idea that is. In the Third World and the East and indigenous cultures of course there is no such thing as an author. They don't have any texts and, if they do, the texts just grow, like grass and trees and the rain forest. They appear, they emanate out of the rocks and plants, the birds and snakes and medicinal herbs and the smoke of the campfire. It's very beautiful.

Ayer, A. J.
A rather dodgy philosopher – much too keen on the VIENNA CIRCLE, LOGICAL POSITIVISM and Tottenham Hotspur. But made up for it by being a sexpot and party animal, and chatting with Mike Tyson.

Bacon, Francis
Horrible man, obsessed with raping Nature. Control freak. Defeated the Spanish Armada.

Balanced
Agreeing with me.

Bashing
Criticising something that I approve of.

Beard
Fashion accessory for the hippest of literary theorists. Probably best not dyed blue though.

Beg the question
A useful tactic when cornered, but hard to get away with. People tend to notice.

Behaviourism
Odious, positivistic notion that psychology should only concern itself with observable behaviour. Of course, what it should really be about are things like feelings, intuition and self-help, but scientistic types worried that these couldn't be measured so they jettisoned them. Happily psychology's more sophisticated cousin psycho-analysis jumped into the breach and now there really is no need for psychology at all.

Benjamin, Walter
By far the hippest member of the Frankfurt School. Committed suicide, for one thing, which is always a dead give-away of hipness. To be sure Benjamin did it to escape the Nazis, rather than because he was bored or alienated or oppressed by his husband or to make an existential statement, so in that sense it was less hip; but still. And he was hipper than ADORNO because he didn't say anything harsh and elitist about jazz or popular culture, and then 1940 was a hipper time to die than 1969 (unless you were Janis Joplin or someone).

Bi-polar disorder
Not so much a disorder, as a lifestyle choice. If a bear wants to swing both ways, why shouldn't it?

17

Bible, the
DERRIDA's *Of Grammatology*.

Bigot
Someone who believes something I don't believe. See FANATIC.

Binary
Terrible, dreadful, shocking word for a truly appalling way to think. Makes everything separate. That must not be. We are all ONE. Everything is One.

Biological
Concept, term, category, frame of reference it is imperative to repudiate. Absolutely nothing is biological. (Except insects, some plants and the spiny anteater; but not viruses and bacteria, which are decidedly socially constructed.) Above all humans are not biological, and to say or think that they are is an absurd mistake. Humans have nothing whatever to do with biology; we are entirely artificial, self-created, invented; we're as made-up as glass or Kleenex or Aspartame. Nothing about us has anything to do with biology, especially not sex, reproduction, child-rearing, aggression, or competition. All of that is entirely cultural and social; none of it is 'hard-wired' or adaptive or understandable in such terms. See ESSENTIALISM, DETERMINISM.

Biopolitics
Foucauldian term for the way governments force people to be healthy. Hospitals are transformed into sinister 'curing machines' instead of just places to hide in when you're sick. Illness becomes a pretext for medical intervention and domestic life is medicalised as people are taught to wash their hands now and then. This neurotic emphasis on hygiene makes medicine an agency of SOCIAL CONTROL.

Bivalence
Somewhat dubious idea that a proposition which makes a truth-claim has to be either true or false. Bivalence is probably half-true. See FUZZY LOGIC.

Body
A thing (*res*) or entity discovered by FOUCAULT (possibly influenced, or rather anticipated, by the work of Merleau-Ponty) and further elaborated by BUTLER. Generally has two arms and two legs, except when it doesn't (see DISABILITY STUDIES). Tends to like sex, also scratching (see ITCH). Between the two legs has genitalia, a sub-topic of Body studies that repays extensive examination. The body is a text that the world inscribes as it pleases, thus is a site of resistance.

Bogus derivation
As Immanuel Kant famously argued, if you want to make a dubious claim, it's going to sound far more convincing if you pretend some luminary has said it before. This is bogus derivation. If you get caught out, you simply say that it wasn't the world authority you were referring to, but rather your next door neighbour, who coincidentally has the same name.

Bonobo
Close relative of the SEA HORSE, Bonobos embrace sisterhood with an admirable militancy and not a few orgasms. Males play no part in the orgasm thing, so there's nothing new there then. Dr Susan Block, whilst urging people to 'liberate their inner bonobo', has pointed out that it isn't possible to fight a war whilst having an orgasm. This explains why no bonobos have been spotted on the front line in Iraq.

Botton, Alain de
Almost certainly, amongst the group of philosophers born in Zurich on 20 December 1969, who then moved to England when

they were eight, and went to Cambridge to study History in 1987, Alain de Botton is not the worst.

Bourgeoisie
Powerful cabal which owns the means of production. This gives it control over the rest of society. It isn't entirely clear whether it realises it has got this control, because there isn't much sign that it exercises it effectively. The rest of society means things like the police, the media and universities. In this respect, it is odd that the bourgeoisie allow radical Theorists to work in universities, but probably it doesn't understand the liberatory power of experimental texts. It would do well to learn the lesson of the Russian revolution. Threaten the masses with *Of Grammatology*, and they'll soon be revolting.

Brain ventricles
Holes in the brain filled with cerebrospinal fluid. Tend to be bigger in people with schizophrenia, probably as a result of too many family arguments about *EastEnders*. See PSYCHIATRY.

Burgess
Famous snail. Prison interrupted a short career in MI5. Wrote *Clockwork Orange* from behind bars. See EVOLUTION.

Burt, Cyril
The man who showed how science is really done.

Butler, Judith
One of the greats. A superstar. Often called a superstar even by the mainstream press, so she's really famous, a household name. Her work is significant, influential, and difficult. Some guy in Oregon said she's one of the smartest people in the world, and he should know. Of course there are jealous people, nobodies and losers like

20

Martha Nussbaum, who say she's difficult to no particular purpose, but they're just jealous. Butler's work is on The BODY, desire, and gender. Her thought is greatly influenced by the fresh, novel, unfamiliar combination of NIETZSCHE, FREUD and FOUCAULT. She is interested in performance and repetition, so her texts perform this interest by way of a heavy use of repetition. In short, she says two or three things over and over again in emptily technical language until she has enough words for a book. This is a massively impressive feat, and that's why she is a household name.

Butterfly
Extremely dangerous, non-linear insect. Studied in the wild by Edward Lorenz – presumably an ancestor of the famous zoologist Konrad Lorenz – who found that it could cause hurricanes and tornados with a flap of a wing. Still slightly less scary than a moth, though. See WEATHER FORECASTING.

Canon, the
A mysterious document (which no one has ever seen) drawn up (no one knows when) in secrecy by a tiny conspiracy (no one knows where) of deceased European males dictating what everyone must read.

Capitalism
Irrational hatred of capital cities. Should be eradicated.

Captive audience
One of the perks of the job.

Carbuncles
1) MARXIST ailment; ITCHY.
2 Architectural feature (see CHARLES).

Carnivore
Animal, once pacifist, but now meat-eating. Change thought to have occurred after exposure to television programmes like *Champion the Wonder Horse* in the 1950s.

Catastrophism
A theory describing what occurs when we're asked to explain our ideas clearly.

Cather, Willa
Novelist. Good because gay, and multicultural. She wrote about immigrants (Swedish, German, Italian, Czechoslovakian, all sorts), Native Americans, Hispanics. Nobody actually reads her novels though, probably because Nebraska is so boring.

Chaos theory
Describes what happens at a MODERN LANGUAGE ASSOCIATION CONVENTION when two delegates turn up wearing the same kind of Manolo Blahnik shoes and reading the same classic edition of LACAN's masterpiece, *Ecrits*. See HISSY FIT.

Charles, Prince
Future monarch and polymath. Expert on architecture, 'complementary' medicine, plant psychology, Laurens van der Post, fast cars, polo, vegetarianism, shooting. See CLASS UP-ITSELF.

Chatterton, Thomas
Poet who killed himself when he was seventeen, setting an all-time record for early achievement of hipness via suicide. Also probably

started the fashion for poets to round off a career (whether short or long) by killing themselves.

Chi-Chi
Famous London Zoo panda, which specialised in bamboo eating and acupuncture. Symbol of diversity and harmonious co-existence of black and white (see BIVALENCE). Had a stutter. See THERAPEUTIC TOUCH.

Circle
Good thing to talk in a.

Class for-itself.
Social class which looks after its own interests. See CLASS IN-ITSELF.

Class in-itself
The working class – or proletariat, if you prefer – has an irritating tendency not to recognise that it carries the hopes of mankind on its shoulders. Indeed, frequently it does not recognise that it is a class at all. This would be embarrassing for Marxist theory were it not for the fact that classes are defined objectively. The working class is what it is whether it likes it or not. It's a class in-itself. It just doesn't know it. It's a bit slow like that. See PROLETARIAT.

Class up-itself
A social class when it gets really smug. See CHARLES, CLASS IN-ITSELF.

Clinic
A place where people are punished for being ill.

Comfortable
A word to use instead of 'agree with', 'accept', 'understand'. 'Doctors have become more comfortable with alternative medicine'.

This is useful in subtly training us to replace out-of-date ways of assessing truth-claims such as logic and evidence with the idea of a nice sofa.

Commodity fetishism
Taking canned goods (corn, green beans, tomatoes, etc) to bed with one.

Complementary medicine
Very polite kind of medicine, probably because of its association with royalty. Has a pathological aversion to placebos and double-blind testing. Its effects are subtle and holistic, so nobody should be surprised that there isn't evidence that it makes people better. Anyway, illness is just a reified social category. Except housemaid's knee, which is really nasty. See ALTERNATIVE MEDICINE, CHARLES, MEDICINE.

Complicated
What to call your work when people like Gross and Levitt don't think much of it. See HIGHER SUPERSTITION.

Conditioned response
Unpleasant things require an automatic negative response. It is possible to condition yourself in order to get such a thing. Here's an example of how you might do it. Retrieve your copy of Alan SOKAL's *Intellectual Impostures* from the bin. Sit down and begin to read it. As you get to a particularly odious section, hit yourself over the head as hard as possible with it. It might also help if you ring a bell at the same time. Repeat this process until you reach the end of the book. You'll then find that the next time somebody mentions Alan Sokal, you'll duck and be instantly struck down by a severe headache. This will remind you that you don't like Sokal, which is very useful. It is also possible that you'll salivate, which isn't so useful, so make sure you carry a handkerchief around with you. See BEHAVIOURISM.

Confirmation bias
Something scientists and positivists worry about a lot, but it just seems like good sense. Who else's bias are you going to follow instead of your own?

Conformity
A deeply divisive phenomenon.

Conservative
Until ten years ago the worst kind of thing to be. Innovation, risk and fissure are the lifeblood of academic progress. However, with the advent of POSTMODERN and DECONSTRUCTIONIST techniques there is now a tradition worth conserving. Especially when one considers that these things are increasingly under attack by reactionaries like SOKAL. Probably the time is ripe for the emergence of a new kind of progress. Something like *progressive statics*. Or *fissure through gradualism*. This would have the advantage of extending the shelf-life of experimental texts.

Conspicuous consumption
1) Phrase coined by Thorstein Veblen to explain why rich people drive expensive cars, wear jewellery, and pretend to like opera. See POSITIONAL GOODS.
2) An extremely thin person with a hacking cough.

Consumerism
The result of REPRESSIVE DESUBLIMATION – after all, you never see a BONOBO with an IPod – consumerism is frankly inexcusable. However, it is important to distinguish between consumerism and its altogether different cousin; fashion. Mill's *Utilitarianism* is key here. Buying a Prada handbag is so obviously a higher pleasure that it cannot possibly be an example of consumerism. Neither can hemp. But Kylie Minogue is a different matter. Very much a lower pleasure.

Conventional

Useful word with which to do two contradictory things at once: to denigrate one's opponents and to cover one's ass. 'Conventional' is a pejorative, but it also acknowledges (in a pejorative way) that one's opponents may have a superficially better case. Thus one may refer to conventional mathematics as opposed to Lacanian mathematics: this simultaneously concedes that Lacanian mathematics is not the kind that engineers and cashiers ought to use, and indicates how dull and conformist such people are. So with conventional science, conventional history, etc.

Conventional mathematics

The kind done by mathematicians as opposed to the kind done by LACAN. Requires the ability to add up.

Copenhagen

Famous quantum city. Rumoured to be in Denmark, though its boundaries are uncertain so probably it's in Sweden as well (see STOCKHOLM). The city frequently comes up in conversation twinned with the word interpretation. This can be slightly scary, since there is a chance that you're talking to a real physicist. If this happens, the best thing to do is to start talking about MERMAIDS by way of a diversion. If your physicist mentions David Bohm, counter with the anti-elitist, Hans Christian Andersen.

Counting

Hugely overrated ability requiring large numbers of fingers.

Creationism

There are those who claim that POSTMODERNISM gives aid and comfort to creationists and supporters of Intelligent Design. It is true that no thinking person can actually believe that God created Homo sapiens as described in the first book of the Bible, of course. But, to the extent that truth is relative to discourses or language games, it isn't quite clear how it is possible to criticise the claims of religion. But one can always point out how conservative creationism is, which surely ought to be decisive. Furthermore, it's based on a misunderstanding of the nature of texts. Texts do not give up their meaning. Interrogate them all you like, they remain fundamentally opaque. This means that the biblical story of creation is an illusion, and creationism must be bunk. There is simply no need for the totalising grand narratives of the ENLIGHTENMENT in order to repudiate creationism.

Credulity
A great virtue.

Crop circles
The work of peasant farmers, crop circles, a special form of crop art, represent the harmonious relationship between tiller and land through a connotative articulation of sphericalness. People who claim that this art form is corny simply don't understand nature and the moon.

Crop yields
Difficult thing, crop yields. On the one hand, it is, of course, desirable that we should at least be able to feed some people by growing crops. But, on the other hand, not if it means that you put peasant farmers out of work. That goes without saying. It is probably best to think of crop-growing as more like a hobby than about feeding the world. After all, it is possible for people to eat things which haven't been grown. Chocolate, for instance. And cheeseburgers. Without the bap. See MONO-CROPS.

Darwin

Primarily an economist, who happened upon the theory of evolution after dabbling on the Stock Exchange. Renowned geneticist Richard Lewontin puts it this way in *Biology as Ideology*: 'Darwin's whole theory of evolution by natural selection bears an uncanny resemblance to the political economic theory of early capitalism... Darwin had some knowledge of the economic survival of the fittest because he earned his living from investment in shares he followed daily in the newspapers. What Darwin did was take early nineteenth-century political economy and expand it to include all of natural economy.' See EUGENICS, GALAPAGOS ISLANDS.

De trop

Opposite of de bottom.

Dead rabbits

Have bright eyes. Tasty. See GARFINKEL, MOA.

Death

To be avoided if possible, except if you're an author, in which case it is essential. Especially if you find you can't stop writing about a boy called Harry.

Death of the author

As Barthes so wisely pointed out in 1968 in 'La Mort de l'auteur', the idea of the author is tyrannical because it confines the text within a single meaning, thus denying the importance of its inter-textuality and imprisoning readers in a narrow oppressive interpretation. The death of the author means the joyous liberation of the reader, who takes advantage of this liberty to interpret every text as an individual utterance of the broader system of class discourse. See NOVEL.

Deconstruction
Method of interrogating texts to see whether they have committed any terrible crimes. Signs of guilt include: sentences that make sense; truth claims; author without a NAZI past; etc.

Deep ecology
Developed by Norwegian philosopher Arne Naess, no relation of the famous monster. Stresses that all beings have equal intrinsic value, though apparently there is some argument over the dung beetle and *Pop Idol* contestants. The philosophy itself is a little confusing, but what can be said with certainty is that throwing stones at local wildlife is a no-no. Damn.

Defensive
Adjective for someone who insists on disagreeing with me, and goes on disagreeing even after I've said how right I am.

Dehydration
An occupational hazard for academics. They have to keep a constant flow of beverages going or they risk abruptly losing consciousness. See LIFE OF RILEY, SOCRATIC DEFORMATION.

Democracy
Means that no one knows more than anyone else about anything (except Theorists, of course, but since they know more than anyone else on behalf of democracy it's all right). No one knows more than anyone else about 'literature', for instance, which is why the NEW CRITICISM was so elitist and bad and is now gone. Democracy also means that no genre or kind of writing (or '*écriture*') or discourse is better than any other, so shopping lists and phone books and *Sports*

Illustrated are just as good as *Hamlet*, exactly the same kind of thing, no difference, equal.

Demonising
Sharply criticising something that I approve of.

Demonstrate
Word to use when you want to claim that someone (FOUCAULT, FREUD, people like that) actually did *discover* something, i.e., had some good evidence, as opposed to just thinking of it and then saying it.

Derrida, Jacques
He invented DECONSTRUCTION. Nothing more need be said. Except that he's got sexy white hair. And he was friendly with Paul de MAN, which caused a little local difficulty. And, of course, there was the whole bust up about the honorary degree from Cambridge. But mainly he invented deconstruction.

Determinism
1)   Irrevocable when biological. Not so when environmental.
2)   An accusation. Normally paired with its twin, REDUCTIONIST. No need to understand what either of these means.

Deviation
A good thing obviously because straight lines, borders, and conformity are all part of the armamentarium of social control.

Dialectical biology
A kind of biology done by people who speak non-standard varieties of English, which are just as good as the standard, no, better, because not so elitist, so the biology is better too.

Dice
God's favourite toy. Mention when talking about QUANTUM things.

Difference
Universally acknowledged to be a good thing. Therefore sameness is a bad thing, therefore the majority way of doing things is not just sometimes but always and necessarily inferior (or 'inferior') to the minority way of doing them. So, eating is inferior to anorexia, and seeing is inferior to blindness, and health is inferior to illness, for example (except possibly in countries where illness is endemic, but then worries about dominant discourses come into play, so the effect is the same). This opens up possibilities for many new kinds of Studies. DISABILITY STUDIES, Eating Disorder Studies, Six Finger Studies.

Difficult
1) Disciplines like physics, mathematics, engineering, which is why I don't want to do them.
2) What to call theoretical work that other people say is incoherent, nonsensical, jargon-ridden and empty.

Disability studies
Exciting new field which, FOLLOWING FOUCAULT, problematises the social construction of disability, using the social construction of race and gender as a model. The field is so exciting and happening that people are having their legs cut off in order to join in.

Discipline
What clinics, hospitals, factories and schools teach. Also a sexual inclination.

Discourse
An alternative (in both senses) way of saying text, or ideology, or

paradigm, or, better yet, all three at once. In other words, a way of deconstructing and subverting, of problematising and putting into question, texts and ideologies and paradigms, with one little word. So talking about the discourse of MEDICINE or law, for instance, right away signals that something sinister is going on with medicine or law, and it's a damn good thing the forces of Theory are on hand to look into the matter.

Displacement activity
It's quite difficult and fatiguing to deal with real problems, so it's much better to challenge bourgeois hegemony by way of the CANON or EUROCENTRISM or similar.

Doctor, medical
Similar to prison guards but allowed to wear a stethoscope.

Dolly the sheep
Freaky sheep, now thankfully dead. Mutton dressed as mutton. Frankenstein's monster in sheep's clothing. All around bad egg. See TWINS. WOOLLY THINKING.

Double-blind testing
Unnecessary experimental technique. Pretty much it is an excuse to withhold medical treatments from half the hospital population. 'Sorry Mrs Jones, I just don't know whether you got the new super drug or the glucose placebo. Yes, I'm sure it's just a coincidence that you look a bit like a sugar frosted donut'. Anyway, let's face it, it's hardly a surprise that doctors don't know what they're up to when they administer a treatment. See PLACEBO.

Doubt
A corrosive poison.

Dowsing

This one is definitely legitimate. People think it isn't, but it is. It works. Nobody knows exactly how aspirin works either, but it still works. With dowsing it's probably some special subset of gravity of some kind. The wood in the forked stick gets just a little bit heavier – the gravitational pull gets just a little bit stronger – when it's in range of water. Perfectly natural and scientific, not woo-woo at all.

Dread

1) Subtly different from angst, which is not quite the same as ANGUISH, which is different from ANOMIE, which is not identical to ALIENATION.
2) Singular of dreads; seldom used.

Dreads

Short for dreadlocks. 'Love your dreads, man,' is a recurrent line of dialogue on *Queer Eye for the Straight Guy*.

Dream

FREUD explained them. Whatever they seem to be about, they're about sex and wanting to kill people really. Except they're also messages from the Beyond or from extraterrestrials.

Druids

Elderly men who look like Merlin, or Gandalf, or maybe EINSTEIN. Lived in Britain a long time ago, when the Celts did, and drank out of beakers. Built STONEHENGE, raised the dead, made CROP CIRCLES, were in touch with Nature.

Durkheim, Emile

French sociologist, almost entirely reprehensible. He was into social stability. Of all things, he thought that the division of labour in society resulted in a form of organic solidarity. By this he meant that after a hard day's work people like nothing more than to go to each other's homes to eat their latest organic vegetables. As a result, they're only too happy to go to work the next day and repeat the process. Now there's nothing wrong with organic food – except for all the creepy crawlies, obviously – but really people shouldn't encourage CAPITALISM by having jobs. If only people were more *engagé*.

E=MC²
Probably a sexed equation, the product of a male obsession with speed. Luce Irigaray explained it this way in 'Le sujet de la science est-il sexue?' 'Is e=mc² a sexed equation?... Perhaps it is. Let us make the hypothesis that it is insofar as it privileges the speed of light over other speeds that are vitally necessary to us. What seems to me to indicate the possible sexed nature of the equation is not directly its uses by nuclear weapons, rather it is having privileged what goes the fastest...'.

Eco, Umberto
Italian structuralist and novelist. Easily confused with Luciano Pavarotti.

Edge
A thing it is necessary to be on the cutting part of.

Edgy
Hip, now, happenin', cool. Not old news, *vieux jeu*, stale, last week, last Thursday.

Edinburgh

City north of London, famous as the home of the STRONG PROGRAMME. Its streets are thronged with muscular sociologists elbowing everyone off the pavement.

Education

Brutal, violent intrusion of arbitrary material into the clean innocent heads of children, which should be left empty.

Efficiency

Faster way of working. See TELEVISION.

Eight Cousins

Louisa May Alcott novel about altruism and self-sacrifice in nineteenth century Boston. See INCLUSIVE FITNESS.

Einstein, Albert

Primarily a patent office clerk, Einstein, feeling jaded at the turn of the twentieth century, and in the run up to the Great War, and in its aftermath, proved that everything is relative in the physical world.

Elitist

Someone who knows more than I do.

Emancipatory ends

What should be the goal of science.

Empiricism

Absurd notion that observation and measurement are useful in finding out about things. See POSITIVISM.

Engels, Friedrich
Manchester industrialist and revolutionary thinker who went on to feature in *A Little House on the Prairie*.

Enlightenment
Sinister, destructive period of history which had a 'project' to dominate nature, prefer reason to superstition, and stop going to church. All a big mistake, but POSTMODERNISM will fix it.

Epistemic freedom
One of the chief dividends of postmodern thought. The realisation that truth is constituted in particular DISCOURSES means that we are all gloriously free to believe whatever we want to. We don't have to stay trapped in scientific or rationalist discourse, we can move over to spiritual discourse, or indigenous mythology discourse, or I saw this on TV and it was interesting and kind of scary discourse, and then we can believe a lot of things that would be forbidden in those narrow reductionist empirical discourses.

Epistemological break
ALTHUSSERIAN notion referencing the broken ankle that Karl MARX suffered after falling off a soapbox when protesting against his own HEGELIAN TENDENCIES.

Epistemology
1) Useful philosophical word to indicate that it isn't possible to know anything. Should be employed as an adjective – epistemologically – with words like unsound, naive and suspect. Need to practise contemptuous look to deal with any clever-clogs who ask how it is possible to know that it isn't possible to know anything. Contemptuous look can be employed together with the word paradoxical in really difficult cases.
2) A way to shift your ground. If someone nails you on

epistemology, say the issue is the social consequences of science. When the coast is clear, say the issue is epistemology.

Eternal recurrence
Nietzschean expression designating the strange phenomenon which makes it seem that every single undergraduate essay is exactly the same. NIETZSCHE believed that it is the ultimate mark of a superman to be able to grade 100 such essays whilst resisting the urge to kill somebody.

Eudaimonia
Usually translated 'flourishing' or 'well-being'. Aristotelian version of happiness. Now understood to include and require the right to believe whatever one likes.

Eugenics
A really bad idea that was very popular about a hundred years ago, to do with 'improving' the population by discouraging or preventing 'inferior' people from 'breeding' via incentives or forced sterilisation. A terrible, racist, cruel idea – but a bit of a godsend in a way, because it's provided a useful weapon against SOCIOBIOLOGY and Darwinism ever since, even though people caught on that eugenics was a truly appalling idea many decades ago, and it has no necessary connection with Darwinism in any case. But hey, Francis Galton was a cousin of DARWIN'S, so it's child's play to blame the whole notion on Darwin and keep on linking sociobiology and Nazism for ever and ever. See HORST WESSEL SONG.

Eurocentrism
Thought-crime, discourse-crime, text-crime, in which people think or talk or write about Europe instead of the Third World. Europe of course includes the US, Canada, Australia and New Zealand. Eurocentrism is endemic among scientists, for example, who never

stop talking about Newton and Aristotle and Darwin and never mention all their many counterparts in Asia and Africa and indigenous cultures. This is a terrible mistake because it ignores and belittles the shining example of the HOLISTIC cultures of the non-European world who wisely decided not to take the path of atomistic, REDUCTIONIST Western science, and are so much happier and more comfortable as a result. Plus of course it's just morally wrong because science and all other forms of thought should be multicultural, which entails equal representation from every culture on earth.

Evidence
1) Something that can be tailored to the requirements of my arguments.
2) A tiresome thing that may conflict with something that I believe.

Evolution
Something to do with a snail called Burgess. Occurred only during the Cambrian period. Punctuated, not smooth.

Exclusion
What happens when you use JUDGMENT, LOGIC, LINEAR THINKING, REASON, ARGUMENT. Very bad and unkind thing to do, especially for women, who are by nature caring and loving, except when we argue with biological determinists, when they're not.

Existenz
Existence, but it sounds like more than that in German.

Experiment
Experimental texts are good. They rely on sensible things like INTUITION, ASSERTION and ATTITUDE. Not that they have authors, of

course. That's what makes them experimental. But experiments in laboratories are bad. They make use of instruments of oppression, like Petri dishes and microscopes. They're also all about controlling things, especially variables . And, of course, there's the HAWTHORNE EFFECT, which has something to do with experiments and the flourishing of trees and forests. This might be thought to be a good thing, until one remembers that just about all trees are now GM trees, and should, therefore, be turned into paper so that we can print out our experimental texts. Doubly so, if they grow in TUSCANY right where someone wants to build a house.

Fairies at the bottom of the garden
Probably not there. Probably a trick of the light, or something about the way delphiniums look after heavy rain. But it's impossible to be sure, no one has actually examined the bottom of every single garden on earth under a microscope, so the question remains open. See ROSWELL.

Falsifiable
A bad thing for a theory or hypothesis to be. Clearly, it's much better if you know for certain that nobody can show that you're wrong. Especially Alan SOKAL. Anyway, frankly you'd have to be on drugs – probably poppers – to think that the notion even makes sense. If there's no truth, then you're not going to get very far trying to falsify things. It is important to remember to say this – lots of times, preferably – if you ever get criticised by a scientist. If this doesn't work, crying can be useful.

Fanatic
Someone who strongly believes something I don't believe.

Fashion
Important ethical principle. Something that is behind the times is very wrong indeed.

Feminism
Another item that depends on location. An excellent thing in the West, but a form of EUROCENTRIC hegemonic discourse in the Third World. Subaltern cultures have their own customs that give them meaning, and if those customs include mutilating or imprisoning or murdering women, that's their business. It's patronising and condescending for Western feminists not to realise that Third World women have agency and are perfectly able to choose to be treated like dirt all by themselves.

Fetish
A nice, comforting object (a shoe, a foot, a dead chicken) that substitutes for the mother's penis and soothes castration anxiety. See MANOLO BLAHNIK.

Feyerabend, Paul
He was a kind of radical Thomas KUHN. He advocated epistemological or methodological anarchism. This involves dressing in black, wearing a little badge with an A on it, waving placards with 'Socialist Worker' written on them, and invading science laboratories. Feyerabend argued that this is a good way of finding things out. Mainly who your real friends are.

Fingers
1) Used for counting.
2) Very useful for scratching. See ITCH.
3) Central to DISABILITY STUDIES, Six Finger Studies.
4) Largely socially constructed, in the manner of race, gender, disability. Granted, most of us are born with them attached to the ends of our hands, but how we think about them, what

we do with them, what other people think about what we do with them, are all socially constructed.

Fissure
A radical break with tradition. A bit like eating turkey at Christmas rather than tofu. Or taking your Italian vacation in Umbria rather than TUSCANY. Or looking interested when an undergraduate student carps about the grade you gave him for his latest essay. Fissure, of course, is to be encouraged. There's no place in this brave new world of innovation and risk for outmoded, cod theories based on a discredited tradition. It's time to slough off the past.

Flaubert, Gustave
Bit of a mixed bag – like so many 'authors'. Hated the bourgeoisie, so that's good. But was a terrible Orientaliser, and a closet Romantic, and thought the Paris communards were idiots. And then his fetishisation of *le mot juste* – what could be more LOGOCENTRIC than that? And he hung with other logocentrists like Henry James and Turgenev – but then James was gay, so there's that – plus Flaubert was great friends with the cross-dresser George Sand. Hard to pin down, in short.

Flow
What to go with.

Fluid
A female thing. Blood, milk, sweat, tears. All exclusive to women. This explains why men are engineers and women work in dairies, laundries, and Mills & Boon.

Following Foucault
1) A popular phrase in sentences that begin 'If, following Foucault, we understand power as etc.' Useful shorthand to

indicate well-trodden path writer is about to take, as well as to indicate loyalties, allegiances, knowingness, Masonic handshake, etc.

2)   A game involving a pendulum played at faculty parties.

Foucault, Michel

French philosopher, inventor and historian of thought. He hoped to develop an 'archaeology of knowledge', which pretty much meant digging up pavements and roads to see whether he could find buried discursive formations. Since he was the only person who had any idea what these might be, nobody can be certain whether he succeeded in his task. However, he was responsible for rolling out cable television in his native Poitiers. He also invented a pendulum, thereby proving that the world rotates.

Free will

Now thought to vary inversely with the number of GENES. Or at least the smaller the number of genes an organism has, the less its behaviour is determined. This has led to the counterintuitive, but indubitable, conclusion that fruit flies have more freedom than human beings. Presumably this means things such as that they don't have to go to work everyday, that they can stay up late watching re-runs of *Dawson's Creek* on a weekday, and they can sleep around without fear of social opprobrium. Oh to be a FRUIT FLY.

Freud, Sigmund

Though he did have some unfortunate ideas about women, he discovered the Unconscious, despite the many people who had pointed out its existence before, so we have to keep paying homage to him.

Friends of the Earth

It is not true that these people are only friends with the earth because nobody else likes them. Oh bugger it, yes it is. See GREENPEACE.

Fruit Fly

Well-dressed insect, with some 13,000 pairs of genes. Often to be found hovering indecisively between an apple and a pear unable to decide which one to eat, behaviour which is thought to have inspired Buridan's ass. See FREE WILL.

Fuzzy logic

Logic done by people who aren't very good at it. Because of the nature of truth and logic, this isn't necessarily a problem. See BIVALENCE.

Galapagos Islands

Original location of Stock Exchange. Relocation to London occurred after invasion by irritating finches. See DARWIN.

Gamete

There are useful gametes, known as ova or eggs, and superfluous gametes, known as sperm. In a better world, there would be billions of ova for every one sperm, but of course in this one it's the other way around. Wouldn't you know it. Another possibility for the better world would be if the two inhabited separate continents and never met, but that's not the case either. Sad to say, there is sex, which causes them to fuse and make more gametes. The only consolation is that millions of the horrid sperm creatures are annihilated in the process, but this fails to console once you realise that ten minutes later there are another million ready to take their place. It can take longer in an older man, though.

Garfinkel, Harold

A sociologist with big hair, he invented ethnomethodology,

persuaded children that they lived in hotels, had a successful career singing about DEAD RABBITS and bridges, and opened a chain of restaurants.

Gender studies

In a bold, daring, risky move, Gender Studies combined Women's Studies with Queer Studies and Men's Studies to create the new umbrella discourse of Gender Studies. The project is to theorise the social construction of gender, to theorise it so exhaustively and thoroughly that no one, not even the most dogmatic, linear, PHALLOGOCENTRIC sociobiologist will ever again think, or say, there are any real or 'natural' BIOLOGICAL differences between males and females. Progress is slow but that's all right - why should speed be privileged? See LIGHT.

Geeky

What to call SOKAL if you're an editor of *Social Text*.

Genes

Do very little. Can be ignored. Not selfish, kind.

Genet, Jean

French novelist and playwright. Once considered very radical and TRANSGRESSIVE, very dangerous and edgy, but he looks pretty tame now compared to Quentin Tarrantino or Takeshi Kitano, so no one bothers to mention him much any more.

Genetic drift

Occurs in humans after a mutation of the gene for swimming (thought to have accounted for the demise of Shelley). See HERACLITUS, SYNCHRONISED SWIMMING.

Genius

Absurd old-fashioned naive idea that individual people come up with brilliant original ideas, which is obviously nonsense. Except of course when it's a question of Nietzsche, Freud, Derrida and Foucault. They're geniuses. The greatest who've ever lived, in fact. And except when it's a matter of Judith BUTLER or Fredric Jameson or Edward Said, who are also geniuses. But no one else is. Maybe a very few other Theorists – but no one else at all.

Gestalt psychology

Holistic psychology, so a good thing. Makes use of what is called Necker Cube therapy. An hour staring at one of those things is enough to encourage anyone to get better.

Globalisation

Synonym for Americanisation. See STARBUCKS.

GM crops

Very dangerous. The safest approach is always to reject all new technology of this sort sight unseen. Keeping existing forms of agriculture in face of rapidly growing global population, of course, not dangerous at all, safe as houses. See TOBACCO.

Goddess

Good, powerful, wise. Until the ALPHABET came along and ruined everything.

Gödel, Kurt

A man with a theorem. Has something to do with axioms. Significantly, shows that everything is relative. To be invoked with QUANTUM things.

Goethe, Johann Wolfgang von

Classic, archetypal dead white guy. Had tendencies to hipness in youth (see WERTHER) but almost immediately turned stodgy, conservative and dull. Worked for the government. As EUROCENTRIC as anyone's ever been – wrote a whole book about his trip to Italy, also endless poems about Greece and Rome. To top it all off he was an arch-Orientaliser. Can't get much worse.

Good breast/Bad breast

Kleinian conception – Melanie, not Calvin – denoting breasts that behave well and badly respectively. The good breast gets along with everyone, is friendly, generous, approachable, looks you right in the eye, and is utterly dependable. The bad breast is aloof, standoffish, sulky, evasive and withholding.

Grade inflation

Failure in education is bad. It's harmful to people's self-esteem, it marks them down as losers and it leads to the suspicion of bad teaching. The solution is to make sure that nobody fails. Hence grade inflation. Critics urge a return to Friedmanesque stringency, but this should be resisted. Anything smacking of Thatcherism just can't be right.

Gramsci, Antonio

Italian Marxist, he went to prison for ten years, came out and promptly died. Despite this carelessness, he made important contributions to Marxist theory. Mainly he pointed out that politics and culture were important. Until Gramsci, it has just been work, work, work with those Marxists.

Greenpeace

How apt that two of the most beautiful words in the English language comprise the name of this wonderful environmental group. Modern day heroes, they spend their time saving WALES, defending us from a GM nightmare, rambling, wearing Wellington Boots and rescuing mice from traps. If you meet a *Greenpeace* activist, it is very important that you don't mention how peculiar it is that the Nazis, of all people, were deeply green. You'd be much better off talking about Gaia, sunsets, healthful ocean cruises and vegan diets. See FRIENDS OF THE EARTH, TABOO.

Ground
Good thing to shift when you're losing an argument. See EPISTEMOLOGY.

Group think
As with so many things, it depends who is doing it. Given the right group, it's a fine and useful thing; with the wrong one, it's obviously a disaster. So it's crucial to choose the right group, and be careful to follow its lead at all times.

Gut
A good part of the body to think with, but not the best. See HEART.

Hale-Bopp
Comet behind which the people in a group (or 'cult') named Heaven's Gate believed a spaceship was hiding. At first glance this seems like an absurd notion, but the fact remains that nobody actually went up there to check. See EPISTEMIC FREEDOM.

Having it both ways
Also known as eating one's cake and having it. On the one hand, repudiating, with disdain and contumely, all forms of hierarchy,

judgment, universalism, totalisation, truth; and on the other hand, judging, condemning, placing at the bottom of a hierarchy, and attributing error to people who disagree with one's views on judgment, truth, universalism, etc.

Hawthorne Effect
Strange effect whereby certain kinds of trees flourish if they're being studied. Well, it's pretty boring being a tree, so probably they put on a bit of an act when they've got an audience.

Head
The wrong part of the body to think with.

Healthy
Unfortunately tame, conformist, predictable state of being. The safe choice. Hard to combine with hipness.

Heart
The right part of the body to think with. See HEAD.

Heaven's Gate
Group of people (mostly computer programmers, bizarrely enough) gathered around a charismatic figure named Marshall Applewhite who believed a spaceship was hiding behind the Hale-Bopp comet waiting to take them to a distant planet. Within this discourse, the way to get from Los Angeles to the spaceship was to dress in new black sweatsuits and commit suicide (no refunds). This all sounds quite loony, and probably is, but there are no objective external criteria by which to establish that it is. One can attempt persuasion, but if that fails, one can only shrug, and perhaps point out that nobody looks good in a sweatsuit.

Hegel, Georg
German philosopher in the idealist tradition. This means that he thought that things like chairs and buses are just special kinds of ideas. It isn't clear whether or not he therefore spent his whole life standing up and insisted on walking everywhere.

Hegelian tendency
A disorder characterised by an unhealthy penchant for metaphysical flights of fancy.

Hegemony
1) The authority or control exercised by our opponents, but never by ourselves.
2) The salary paid to topiarists.

Heidegger, Martin
Very difficult, obscure, profound philosopher, a model for us all. Talked about *Dasein*, and *Sein* and *Zeit*, and authenticity. Had an inappropriate professor-student relationship with Hannah Arendt that influenced the whole course of post-War philosophy, and probably the Cold War as well. Influenced Sartre and all his crowd. Also was a bit too chummy with the NAZIS, but there's no need to dwell on that. See OBSESSIVE.

Heisenberg, Werner
German physicist who kept getting different numbers every time, depending on where he was when he measured. So he realised that mathematics cannot escape the contamination of the social, and discovered the uncertainty principle. Also invented the airship, a technology that was shelved after the fiery Heisenberg crash in New Jersey in 1937.

Hell

Other people, especially if they're ill-dressed. See MANOLO BLAHNIK, SARTRE.

Heraclitus

Early Greek philosopher years ahead of his time. Famed for his doctrine of flux and saying that it isn't possible to drown in the same river twice. More excitingly – though there is some tedious, pedantic arguing about exactly what he meant – he advocated the unity of opposites. What does this mean? Well, imagine a cat sitting on a mat. Could it also be sitting on a settee? Heraclitus thought it could, though it isn't entirely clear whether he thought the mat itself was on the settee.

Herbs

The best medicine. Natural, organic, pure, wholesome. Can cure everything. Western medicine ignores herbs, preferring artificial chemical substances made in test tubes no one knows how. Herbs are much better because not chemical – chemicals of course are toxic.

Hierarchy

A highly suspect category. People who accept it are the lowest of the low.

Higher Superstition

Embarrassing, absurd, na ve book by two POSITIVISTS, Paul Gross and Norman Levitt, who are still intent on defending the exploded notion that science can tell us truths about the world. To read it is to cringe. Gross and Levitt misread and misunderstand people like Andrew Ross, Sandra Harding, Bruno Latour and Stanley Aronowitz and then hold up their misreadings for their scientistic friends to laugh at. Laugh they did, of course, but the rest of the academic community just turned away in shame. Gross and Levitt quote Andrew Ross saying that science functions as an elitist border patrol to keep New Age spirituality out of its laboratories. They seem to find this an outrageous statement; but is it untrue? And that's the pattern for the book as a whole. The powerful insights of the philosophy and sociology of science are taken out of context and ridiculed, but these disciplines attract tens or even hundreds of students every year, so how risible can they be?

Hissy fit
More common than one might think in the academic world. Can be caused by: research assessment exercises; early morning classes; locks on the stationery cupboard; middle of the day classes; overhead projectors; late afternoon classes; students; and colleagues. Happily it is possible to get over hissy fits by drinking copious amounts of tea during the long hours in between seeing students. See LIFE OF RILEY. See DEHYDRATION.

Historical materialism
Materialism from the past. People would covet things like the sharpest flint, woolliest woolly mammoth, biggest cave and gaudiest cave painting. Obviously, there was less materialism back then. Not because there were fewer things to be materialist about, but because they had other, more spiritual priorities. A moon to be prayed to, that kind of thing.

History
Pathetic deluded discipline and project that is somehow blithely unaware of the difficulty of evaluating and interpreting evidence of the past, that just thinks there are a lot of established unquestionable facts and that's all there is to it. Foucault and New Historicism have pointed out these naive errors, so theorists understand, but historians are still clueless.

Holistic
Everything good. Whole, pure, sincere, whole, integrated, spiritual, whole, centred.

Homeopathy
A kind of ALTERNATIVE or COMPLEMENTARY MEDICINE that works better the more diluted it is. It works best if there is none of the medicine left at all. This is effective because the medicine 'remembers' that it was once there, or the water that does the diluting remembers that the medicine was there, or both. So the best method of medicating is to pour a few drops into a river then walk briskly three miles upstream and drink some water there. (It is also possible that the medicine works by association, because the word 'homey' is comforting and reassuring [except when used by heavily armed men].)

Homer
Author, from the days when texts had authors, of Greek epic adventures. Suffers from jaundice. Now resides in Springfield, Illinois. See POLYPHEMUS, THEODICY.

Homework
Something no child should ever have to do. It's bad for their SELF-ESTEEM, and it's too DIFFICULT and takes way too much time when they ought to be watching TV and talking on the phone the way children always have.

Hormones
People in their late teens and early twenties have a lot of them and are not quite used to them yet. This contributes to the CAPTIVE AUDIENCE effect (see UNDERGRADUATES). Used to contribute to academics' sex lives, too, especially the males', but that has become risky now.

Horst Wessel Song

Rumoured to be the song that some SOCIOBIOLOGISTS most like to sing. See NAZI.

Hospital

A place where people are punished for being ill by being made iller.

Human Gnome Project

Most likely something to do with genetic engineering. Probably the idea is to create a new race of tiny human beings.

Human nature

Fantasy. Fictitious entity, like Santa Claus or the tooth fairy or the free lunch. Humans have no nature, only culture; we can learn to fly, or live in the ocean, or echolocate, or pick things up with our trunks, if we will only concentrate.

Hydro-Electric power

The hydro part, excellent. The electric part, not so good. Hydro-Hydro power would be better, but your appliances would get wet. See PSYCHIC PRESSURE.

Hypochondriasis

Hypochondriacs have an abnormal, long-term preoccupation with the possibility that they'll be objectified and oppressed by medical science. Admittedly, it does then seem odd that they spend all their time in doctors' waiting rooms. But this is probably a case of better the devil you know than the devil you don't. Except if the devil is some terminal illness. Which it always is, of course. See ILLNESS, MEDICINE.

Hypothesis
A good or bad thing depending on the context. If the word is being used to mean something like whimsy, then every text should be chock-a-block with hypotheses. But if the word is being used in its POSITIVISTIC sense to mean a proposition or theory which can be tested, then that's bad, very bad. In fact, it's only a stone's throw (see DEEP ECOLOGY) away from full-blown scientism, an offence punishable by the confiscation of all texts by DERRIDA.

Iatrogenesis
Term to describe the process whereby medical science deprives people of the illnesses which are rightfully theirs. It's hardly believable that organisations such as Rotary International want to eradicate disease from the world. Diseases are for life, not just for Christmas. See ILLNESS, MEDICINE.

Ideal speech situation
Concept developed by Habermas to denote the ideal situation in which to give a speech. It includes things like: slavishly attentive audience; absence of PREMATURE EXPOSTULATION; no undergraduates present; lectern decorated with a bit of ethnic embroidery (see ART); ready supply of Perrier water; and after speech party, replete with groupies. Unfortunately, ideal speech situations do not guarantee ideal speeches, but hey there's always the lectern to admire.

Identical twins
Not identical at all. Chalk and cheese.

Ideology
Ideas we don't agree with. Probably exploitative.

Illness

What men do to women, the West to everybody else, invaders to indigenous people, cats to mice, capitalism to us all, meat eaters... oh, you get the idea. See MEDICINE.

Inclusive

The best attitude to everything, including ideas. Accept, welcome, embrace, be kind. Be loving and accepting of everyone, except of course LINEAR THINKERS, REDUCTIONISTS, DETERMINISTS and anyone else whose opinions are dangerous.

Inclusive fitness

1) Absurd idea from evolutionary biology that people should sacrifice themselves for two siblings, four nephews or EIGHT COUSINS. But suppose you're an only child and you don't have cousins or nephews, what do you do then? Are you denied the right to sacrifice yourself? That would be discriminatory. People should be able to sacrifice themselves for any combination of relatives that they choose. Except second cousins, who should sacrifice themselves for anyone who asks them to. See DARWIN.

2) A caring, compassionate, multicultural kind of fitness.

Incompleteness theorem

1) Something GÖDEL said that has to do with saying you can't prove or disprove something, so it's great that a mathematician thought of it even though mathematicians are so GEEKY and POSITIVIST, but they are very useful for giving an air of authority and infallibility to big ideas we want to make huge woolly vague statements about. So incompleteness is like Relativity that way. It just sounds right, it sounds big and general and human conditiony – kind of existential, only newer. We're all incomplete, things are incomplete, things fall apart, the centre cannot hold. And there's sex of course –

incompleteness comes in very handy there.

2) Proves everything is incomplete (see QUANTUM, RELATIVITY) anyway, so I can leave my projects unfinished.

Inferior
A deeply troubling word, obviously, that needs to be problematised, and for preference done away with entirely. And yet so many things are in fact inferior – SCIENCE, REASON, POSITIVISM, LOGOCENTRISM, Western medicine, the list is endless – that it's very difficult to know what to say instead. Maybe inverted commas will have to do. 'Inferior'.

Influence
(verb) An activity that goes in only one direction. Theorists influence others, but no one influences Theorists; they think of everything on their own. NIETZSCHE and FREUD are either partial exceptions to this, or very early theorists themselves. See ANTICIPATE.

Influential
Very useful modifier to use of Theorists, when other modifiers such as clear or well argued won't quite do. Theorists are indeed undeniably influential; lots of people imitate them.

Innovation, Risk and Fisher
Trendy law firm.

Insightful
Thinking pretty much the same way as I do. See BALANCED.

Instinct
A very bad thing when we're discussing evolution, genetics, human nature, but a very good thing when we're discussing women's different ways of knowing.

Intelligence Quotient

A modernist idea invented by a French guy (apparently they weren't quite so cutting edge then) at the beginning of the twentieth century. Goes with the whole empiricist, POSITIVIST way that modernists insist on thinking – the emphasis on measuring and counting everything. Also dovetails neatly with the need to create HIERARCHIES so that people can be sorted and controlled – a very modernist project. The idea is that intelligence is a quantity that can be measured as easily as a body can be weighed, whereas in reality of course it's more like spirit or beauty or irritation, all of which are pretty hard to count (see WISDOM). Fortunately we don't need to worry about IQ too much any more, because Howard Gardner discovered the SEVEN TYPES OF INTELLIGENCE, which shows that intelligence is perfectly evenly distributed. No one has the same amount of all seven kinds, and no one has a lot of all seven, and everyone has a lot of at least one, so the result is everyone is equally intelligent, only in different ways, which is good because it promotes diversity. There is musical intelligence, and emotional, and kinetic, as well as the usual old verbal and mathematical which the IQ test measures. And two more.

Interesting

What the world becomes when you can believe anything you want to. See FREEDOM.

Interrogate

A certain way of reading a text. It involves sitting in a dark-room with a very bright light shining at the text. If it doesn't cooperate, you may want to adopt a good-cop, bad-cop strategy to see if you can get it to give up its secrets. 'Come on text, be a good chap, and I'll let you have a cup of tea'. 'Right you 'orrible little text, tell me what you know else you're gonna get a beatin'.' It's best if you adopt a cockney accent whilst playing the bad cop. Make sure there are no *Amnesty International* activists within earshot while you're doing this kind of thing. Actually, it's probably best if there is nobody at all within earshot. See PSYCHIATRY, TEXT.

Intolerance
Subjecting my assertions or beliefs to criticism.

Intrusion
Disagreement with someone else's belief system, correction of factual error, questioning of an assertion; in general, elitist interference with people's right to believe whatever they like. See JUS CREDERE.

Intuition
A technique for coming to know things about the world. Most fruitfully employed by women. See HEART.

Inverse proportion
Between reliability of findings and finder's need to convince.

Irony
A useful escape mechanism if one is accused of misunderstanding or missing the point – one simply says 'Of course that passage is heavily ironic' with a pitying smile and all will be well.

Is/ought gap
A good place to buy jeans, or do I mean genes?

Itch
An activity or desire or drive of the BODY. A kind of absence or gap or lack which requires to be filled with scratching. Similar to the sex drive or libido except that there are no novels or movies about it. See SNEEZE.

James, Henry

American novelist and transatlantic pseud. Classic dead white guy, in a way. Wrote long novels with very long sentences all about the lily-white upper classes, wore a suit and tie all the time, was always visiting posh friends at places like Chatsworth, turned up his nose at popular culture, was a famous snob, poseur, LOGOCENTRIST, reactionary, duchess-chaser. But on the other hand he was gay, so worth a look.

Jargon

An absolutely essential tool of scholarship, particularly literary criticism. People like to complain about jargon-ridden literary criticism, and claim there is no need for octosyllabic neologisms in order to analyse *Hamlet* or *Wuthering Heights*, but of course that is just white male privilege talking. All scholarship needs jargon. It can't function otherwise. As physicists talk about quarks and leptons, so literary critics talk about narrativity and liminality. It's exactly the same sort of thing, no difference whatsoever.

Jeremiad

Oration or polemic that attacks something I don't want to see attacked.

Jonestown

What happens when attempts to keep up with the neighbours get out of control.

Jouissance

French for lots of fun.

Journal
A place where I write down all my ill-formed thoughts of a night.
See JOURNAL, ACADEMIC.

Journal, academic
A place where I write down all my ill-formed thoughts of a night.
See JOURNAL.

Journalist
1) Tool of bourgeois HEGEMONY, lackey.
2) Exposer of lies and corruption in high places, pillar of democracy and unmasker of sinister designs of scientists. We wouldn't know the awful truth about GM CROPS, the MMR vaccine, the cover-up at ROSWELL, the dangers of electric power lines, and so on, if it weren't for journalists.

Judgment
Bad, wicked, excluding, discriminatory attitude to other people's ways of knowing.

Jung
The right kind of scientist, one with insight and INTUITION and spiritual, albeit highly implausible, ideas, such as the Collective Unconscious.

Junk DNA
The kind of DNA that you leave in an attic to be thrown away when you're spring cleaning. Probably a gift from a well-meaning but evolutionarily challenged grandparent. It turns out that much of DNA is junk. But then that's to be expected when you've only four letters to work with. Even Shakespeare would have struggled, though the typing monkeys would have found things a bit easier. Anyway, all this junk DNA means that human beings don't have

many genes, only about 30,000. This is very good news because it means that like the FRUIT FLY we have free will.

Jus credere
The right to believe.

Kafka, Franz
Brilliantly paranoid, very thin (see CONSPICUOUS CONSUMPTION) novelist and story-writer. Understood about domination, HEGEMONY, persecution, authority, absurdity – had all the makings of a really good Theorist. The one about the cockroach is disgusting. See PRAGUE.

Kantata
The Critique of Pure Reason to music. It hasn't charted yet.

Klein, Melanie
Austrian psychoanalyst, who used FREUDIAN techniques to analyse children. This required the development of a terribly small couch. And also children with a lot of pocket money. Klein was also a pioneer of OBJECT RELATIONS THEORY. This is probably because there are only objects left to have relations with if it gets out that you've been fleecing small children of their pocket money. She had some interesting ideas such as the MATERNAL PENIS and Mammary Manichaeism (see GOOD BREAST/BAD BREAST), but she disagreed with some of Freud's ideas and actually developed her own ideas as modifications of his. That sort of thing is all right for LACAN, but Klein wasn't French.

Knowing
Something women have a special way of.

Knowledge
A human convention subject to fashion, so likely to become out of date quickly, like clothes and shoes and hair styles.

Kuhn, Thomas
A somewhat contradictory figure. He originally trained in theoretical physics, which is bad, but became a philosopher of science, which is good. He wrote *The Structure of Scientific Revolutions* (good), came up with the notion of a scientific paradigm (good) and inspired many of the people working in the sociology of knowledge (good). However, he thought that science can be normal (bad) and that scientific progress is possible (bad). He also wrote books about the history of quantum mechanics (good), which nobody read (bad).

Laboratory
1) A place where scientists gather to torture, bully, extort and rape nature.
2) A place where scientists gather to concoct their stories.
3) The name of a kind of coat, as in Nehru jacket, Mao jacket, kaftan, etc.

Lacan, Jacques
Psychoanalyst with an imaginary penis. Or an imaginary psycho-analyst with a real penis. One of those.

Lamarckism

The great idea that it is possible to pass on to our offspring those characteristics we acquire in our life times. Like, for example, the ability to write experimental texts or to drive sport utility vehicles. This is a good idea because it suggests the possibility of the perfectibility of people kind. Just imagine a world where everybody is able to drive a SUV. Unfortunately, some scientists suggest that Lamarckism might not be right in all its details. But there is no good reason to allow a scientist to ruin a good idea. Just ask the guys at the old *Lenin Academy of Agricultural Science*, they'll tell you. See LYSENKO.

Language game

Something like Scrabble or Boggle. A language game will always have rules. For example, in Scrabble, you're not allowed to whack your opponent over the head with the board if she gets a triple word score (although there may be special dispensation if she's looking really smug about it). It doesn't follow, of course, that everybody will know the rules of language games. So you'll always find some clown who thinks that the Scrabble experience is enhanced if he pinches other people's letters, makes up non-existent words, uses his own 'special' dictionary, that kind of thing. It is, of course, quite within at least the spirit of the rules of Scrabble to hit this type of person with whatever is to hand. See HISSY FIT.

Late monopoly capitalism

Differs from early monopoly capitalism in having a starting point some years after the starting point of the latter.

Lexicography

The kind of thing done by smart-alecks with too much time on their hands. Anyway the whole idea that words have determinate meanings is just so *passé*. The world has no need of dictionaries. Let the play of the signs begin. See SAUSSURE.

Life of Riley
It is tempting to think that long holidays, short hours and non-stop beverages mean that the life of an academic is all too easy. This is not the case. Long holidays are for research. It just happens that academics work at their best whilst in TUSCANY for the summer. Short hours are indicative of the huge amounts of concentration required to come up with a new TRANSGRESSIVE text every decade or so. And as for beverages, well you try staying awake whilst talking to an undergraduate. See DEHYDRATION.

Light
Notoriously sexist phenomenon, privileged because of its position at the very top of the speed-hierarchy. Since speed is a guy thing, so is light (plus it's dark inside women). That EUROCENTRIC Orientaliser GOETHE actually wanted more of the stuff — he was so obsessive that he was fretting about it in his last minutes. Is that pathetic or what. And there's the En*light*enment of course, the ultimate totalising Eurocentric project. The hell with 'more light', more darkness is what's needed. See $E=MC^2$.

Linear thinking
Unfortunate, controlling, impoverished, male variety of thinking that's all hung up on LOGIC, EVIDENCE, chronology, causation, and pedantic in-the-head stuff like that.

Literally
How to take scientists when they claim they're talking metaphorically.

Literary agent
Sells texts without authors to publishers for ridiculously large sums of money. Often lives at the edge and wears a silly hat.

Location

1) Important variable whenever one is counting or measuring something. The numbers are always different in different places.
2) Important in real estate and the restaurant business, too.

Locomotion without a goal

Also known as *dérive* or drift. Kinetic behaviour that lacks a purpose, e.g. skipping, dancing, gesticulating, pretending to aim a kick at someone but not actually landing a kick. See SUDORIC DRIVE.

Logic

Pestiferous male invention. Probably something to do with imperialism, too.

Logical positivism

Extreme confidence in one's own reasoning ability. Normally a Germanic kind of thing, though some Brits have adopted airs and graces in this regard. See VIENNA CIRCLE.

Logocentrism

1) The meaning of 'logocentrism' is not entirely clear to anybody. It has something to do with a tendency to favour speech over the written word. Speech is supposedly all about immediacy, presence and transparency, whereas the written word is about deception and uncertainty. It isn't quite clear who thought these things, but PLATO has been identified as a prime suspect. Anyway, the fact is that neither speech nor the written word is able to get to grips with the nature of the world. If you think that they are, then you're guilty of logocentrism. Probably.
2) A corporate entity can be said to be logocentric if it is willing to spend vast sums of money on a logo which looks as if it has been drawn by a child.

Logorrhea

A common affliction; the Black Lung or RSI of academics. See SOCRATIC DEFORMATION.

Lombroso, Cesare

Italian criminologist who employed scientific techniques in order to demonstrate that scientific techniques should not be employed to study human behaviour. He argued that criminals were victims of evolutionary atavism. This isn't possible because criminality is a social construction. Society causes criminality by defining and labelling certain actions as criminal. If there were no society, there would be no crime. Lombroso should have been locked up for suggesting otherwise.

Lyotard, Jean-François

Very important French philosopher. Invented POSTMODERNISM. Nothing to do with aerobics.

Lysenko, Trofim

Hero of Soviet science, who understood that it is important not to let science get in the way of politics. Sandra Harding expresses this simple truth as follows: 'If a theory "forced" one to assent to politically distasteful, depressing, and counterintuitive claims, then one could regard those consequences as in themselves good reasons to find the theory implausible.' Lysenko followed this logic in his rejection of Mendelianism, and we should celebrate him for it. See LAMARCKISM, MENDEL.

Mack, John

Harvard psychologist who investigates the phenomenon known as alien abduction. He has interviewed a large number of people (a statistically significant number) who give detailed accounts of being visited in the middle of the night by creatures who look exactly like the aliens in *Close Encounters of the Third Kind*, being taken on to an extraterrestrial vehicle, having their genitals and reproductive organs thoroughly explored, and being impregnated. Mack points out that these abductees have intense, even overpowering emotions – fear, excitement, disgust, surprise, consternation – about these events, and that such intense emotion is evidence of the veracity of their accounts. See ROSWELL.

Male

Rational, independent, autonomous, strong, assertive, definite, precise, objective. Some people, even some women, say those are good qualities, universal qualities, that we should all aspire to, whether we have them by nature or have to work for them. But of course that's not right. Those are strictly male attributes, and no one should aspire to them.

Man, Paul de

Belgian journalist, then literary critic/theorist who cleverly employed DECONSTRUCTIONIST techniques, thirty years before deconstruction was invented, whilst writing Nazi propaganda during the Second World War. Even more cleverly neglected to tell anybody what he'd been up to in the war. Chief claim to fame now is as source of urban argot phrase 'You de *man*,' which means 'You have just done something exceptionally clever and impressive.'

Manolo Blahnik

Shoe designer whose products academics don't wear much – except perhaps at the MODERN LANGUAGE ASSOCIATION CONVENTION. See SNAPPIEST DRESSERS.

Marcuse, Herbert

A great guy (despite puzzling lack of profile). Thought up both REPRESSIVE DESUBLIMATION and REPRESSIVE TOLERANCE, which between them pretty much kept the New Left going into the 1970s. They're very useful ideas because they show that the more sex, money, fun, self-expression, play, and time on a luxury yacht you're getting, the worse off you are, which is why a New Left is better than an Old one. Plus Marcuse talked about the liberation of the drives, which opened up the whole new field of drive studies.

Marx, Karl

People who think they have a sense of humour, but do not, would more than likely do a Marx Brothers joke at this point, and it would probably be about as funny as spending a whole night at the opera. But Karl was a serious political thinker, so he shouldn't be joked about. He was very fluential in his day. In fact, despite an unfortunate affinity for grand narratives, he is still influential in some quarters. The clash between anti-totalizing POSTMODERNISTS and pro-totalizing Marxists has enlivened many a conference and curriculum meeting. It's a little sad that Marx missed his calling though. If he'd realised that literary theory was his real talent, he probably would have been more fulfilled, and not had carbuncles. His grandsons were more cheerful that way: they had considerable success in vaudeville and then Hollywood.

Marxism

1)   Probably not true, but it should be.
2)   Useful for understanding dialectical biology.

Masochism

Reading one of our own experimental texts.

Maternal penis

Elusive, tantalising item that causes fetishism.

Mathematics
Who cares. One, two, three, four, whatever. Big, big deal.

Matriarchy
The original way humans organised their affairs until the androcentric Aryans dropped in from central Asia somewhere and deposed all the goddesses and queens and installed Zeus instead. Silly move. The goddesses and queens were so powerful that they decided it was beneath them to resist or do anything about it afterwards, so it's just been all Zeus all the way ever since.

Mead, Margaret
Anthropologist who showed once and for all that humans are infinitely variable, depending on where they live. She studied cultures in the Pacific Ocean somewhere in which men took care of babies, cooked, and put ribbons in their hair, and women cut down trees, killed animals, and spat.

Means of production
The tools and raw materials of production. So we're talking about pens, paper, word processors, tea, furrowed brows, waste-bins, words, coffee, house in Tuscany, that kind of thing. See Proletariat.

Measurement
Tedious, pedantic activity engaged in by scientists because they have nothing better to do. They need to get a life.

Medicine
Bad when Western, good when Eastern or alternative. Admittedly, it's a bit off that Chinese medicine is pretty much the bits of tigers, but hey who's going to miss the odd tiger or two. In its Western form, medicine is an oppressive, objectifying discipline designed to

foster the illusion that illness, disease and death are bad things to be resisted. This, of course, is nonsense. A good dose of smallpox has never done anybody any harm. Except the dodo, maybe. See ALTERNATIVE MEDICINE, COMPLEMENTARY MEDICINE.

Mendel
A monk famous for his love of peas and hatred of blending. His main claim to fame is that he showed how the environment cleverly remembers to influence a child in the same way as it influenced the child's parents. His son was a famous composer. See GENES, HUMAN NATURE.

Mendelssohn, Felix
Cheerful composer with one blue eye and one brown. See MENDEL.

Mermaid
1) Highly interesting and provocative example of liminality and hybridity. Important site for problematisation of woman-fish interface or threshold or border, and examination of social construction of categories 'woman,' 'fish,' and 'mermaid.' See COPENHAGEN.
2) Assisted one of the three wise men.

Metaphor
1) What to call nonsense when someone challenges you on it. 'I'm using quantum metaphorically in that passage.' The rest of the time, of course, you mean it literally.
2) Scientists never talk metaphorically (see FREUD, LITERALLY).

Microscope
A tool that scientists use to peer at tiny powerless things which are none of their business.

Middle Ages

The good times. Before repression, domination, social control, ALIENATION, angst. No technology, no consumerism, no STARBUCKS or Safeway, no indoor plumbing, no outdoor plumbing, no hospitals, no police. Plenty of plague, woodsmoke, pulmonary disease, toothache, priests, robbers, mud, and staggering levels of boredom.

Midgley, Mary

A philosopher who proved beyond a shadow of a doubt that genes don't have emotions (see QUIXOTE).

MMR

Inject if you want to be really good at mathematics.

Moa

Large, selfless, tasty, flightless birds who committed suicide *en masse* so that the kindly Maoris would have a ready supply of roast Moa when they arrived in New Zealand.

Modern Language Association Convention

Great annual US gathering of the peoples; takes place in December in 'convention week' when everyone feels sick after Christmas. Used to be a gathering of literary critics but that was pretty boring, so now it's a gathering of Theorists, which is almost unendurably exciting. Though not for the 90 percent of attendees who are there in hopes of finding a job, nearly all of which are disappointed.

Modesty

A hallmark of literary theorists. *The Columbia Dictionary of Modern Literary and Cultural Criticism*, edited by Joseph Childers and Gary Hentzi, exemplifies modesty in this comment: 'In recent years, the fastest growing, most provocative, and potentially farthest-reaching specialty in the humanities and social sciences has been literary and cultural criticism and theory.'

Mono-crops
Crops which have been modified genetically to be completely devoid of colour. Obviously the result of the HEGEMONY of global agribusiness. Probably not very nutritious, so don't believe people when they tell you that black and white crops are the way to go to feed the world. Colourful crops grown by peasant farmers are much better. So what that there aren't enough to go around. See CHI-CHI, CROP YIELDS, GM CROPS.

Mozart
Composer whose childhood achievements demonstrate what can be accomplished with a decent education. Hollywood has it that he was murdered by fellow composer Antonio Salieri who was annoyed that he hadn't been to quite such a good a school as Mozart.

Multiple personality disorder
Not really a disorder as such, more a tactic. To be a cutting edge Theorist, it is necessary to play multiple roles. Charismatic orator, concerned tutor, pensive intellectual, passionate lover, they're all part of the Theorist's armoury. It is very important not to get mixed up about which role you're playing. Your lover is not going to be too happy, for example, if you burst forth with 'Friends, Romans, Countrymen' just as, in the dim light, you're beginning to look vaguely attractive. See PREMATURE EXPOSTULATION.

Mystery
A beautiful thing. Mystery is always better than understanding. The more obscure everything is, the better.

1970
Turning point year. When it all began. A few brilliant people suddenly discovered the truth about everything and published it, the scales fell from everyone's eyes, and nothing was ever the same after that. By an odd coincidence, most Theorists got their PhDs right around that time.

Name-brand theory
Theory done by stars or superstars, as opposed to generic theory done by people who quote superstars heavily but are not superstars themselves.

Narrative
It's all narrative. Get real, of course it is. All that stuff about evidence and LOGIC is just window dressing, we all know that. Just a way for scientists to puff up their pathetic little egos. They're just spinning a tale like everyone else.

Native rights movements
Movements which have emerged – mainly in Canada it seems – to defend the rights of indigenous people. The basic idea is that governments aren't allowed to build large roads through ancient burial grounds. They're also not allowed to pinch any bones which might possibly belong to some long lost ancestor of an indigenous person. Even if closer examination of the bones in question suggests that the indigenous person's grandmother must have been a fur seal. Which, of course, if their folk history suggests it, is quite possible. See ANCESTOR.

Natural selection
Occurred in the gaps between meteorites. See PUNCTUATED EQUILIBRIUM.

Nature
A beautiful, spiritual thing, to be treated with great respect, except when we really do need to buy a Sport Utility Vehicle, but Nature will understand.

Nazi
The ultimate pejorative, the all-time great, the show stopper. You can use it on SOCIOBIOLOGISTS, REDUCTIONISTS, people who defend science, and Darwinists. If they protest, there is always EUGENICS to fall back on. The one danger in this tactic is that some of those Darwinists and similar people may turn it back around and use it on you. They may bring up HEIDEGGER, or NIETZSCHE, or Paul DE MAN, or DEEP ECOLOGY. They may say, in unpleasant tones, that these connections are a lot more real than those between sociobiology and eugenics. You can try humming a few bars of the HORST WESSEL SONG, or maybe letting your arm rise up in the air a little, or ask how the Volkswagen is driving these days, but the truth is it probably won't help. That's when it's time to remember that you're late for the opera.

Negation of the negation
Hegelian expression indicating that it is possible to get something right by getting it wrong twice. This is very useful if you're the kind of person who gets a lot of things wrong.

Neutral theory of evolution
If you put your car into neutral and step on the accelerator, you don't get anywhere. This pretty much sums up the neutral theory of evolution. Genes frequently just drift about. They're not interested in getting fit. They're certainly not going to go through

any selection process. And they're much too lazy to be selfish. Probably they'll end up on a humanities course at Harvard. See GENETIC DRIFT.

New Criticism

Ordinarily of course 'New' is a hurrah-word, heralding innovation, risk and fissure, a break with tradition, and basic hipness. But in the case of New Criticism the very opposite is true, especially now, when New Criticism is older than STONEHENGE. This is a little frightening if you think about it, so it's best not to.

New Historicism

Not really a fully theorised discipline or theory. Actually just refers to the fact that some literary critics got more interested in history than they had been before.

Newton, Isaac

Like Bacon, an advocate of raping Nature. Also a pitiful has-been. Inventor of a pathetic outdated unhip linear kind of mathematics and astronomy-type thing that worked okay for a couple of centuries but has now been completely left behind, because during the time that everyone was so fed-up after the 1914-18 War, the *Zeitgeist* came up with quantum mechanics, and after that poor old Newton looked very obsolete indeed. Shows you can never be too careful about keeping up.

Nietzsche, Friedrich

German philologist and philosopher. Famed for introducing the idea of superman. As far as we know, Nietzsche's version didn't wear tights and a cape, though who knows what he got up to in the privacy of his own bedroom. Nietzsche also claimed that God is dead. However, some scholars now think that what he meant to say was that his pet dog, Dionysus, was dead. It's an easy mistake to make.

Nitpicking
What to accuse people of when they say you have your facts wrong.

Nothing
A profoundly frightening and disturbing thing or item or object, except of course it can't be any of those because it's the negation of them (and of all the others too) – which is why it's so frightening. A void, an emptiness, a vacuum, a wondering where everything got to. If you're expecting to see a house, a duck, a potato, a lug wrench, and it's not there, what you see instead is Nothing, so naturally that produces Angst. Gnomic announcements like 'Nothing is wrong,' 'Nothing is going to happen,' 'There's Nothing to worry about,' 'Don't be so stupid there's Nothing under the bed' keep us all in a constant state of dread.

Noumenal world
The world in-itself, which, as Kant demonstrated, is unknowable. This means, for example, that if you're mown down by a 213 bus, you can't be sure that you weren't actually hit by a 716 bus. Except, of course, that the 213 is red and the 716 is green. But that probably isn't the point. They didn't have buses in Kant's day. See Phenomenal world.

Novel
A kind of text which transforms ideologemes into individual utterances of the broader system of class discourse.

Obfuscation
Useful move when talking to people who know more than you do.

Object relations theory

Developed by, amongst others, analysts Melanie Klein and D. W. Winnicott, object relations theory concerns the possibility of relationships in a world of OBJECTIFICATION. By means of its techniques, an analysand will learn to recognise, for example, whether they are having a relationship with a Harrods' chaise longue or a Woolworth's lampshade. In this respect, perhaps the major clue identified by ORT is that it is a lot harder to sit comfortably on a lampshade than a chaise longue. Unless you have pleasingly atypical buttocks.

Objectification

To be turned into an object. This is bad because most people end up being turned into something quite inappropriate. A beautiful chaise longue from Harrods, no problem, but who wants to be lampshade from Woolworths? Except maybe somebody attracted to bright lights. See BUTTERFLY.

Objectivity

A bad, male thing, obviously, because people are not objects.

Obscurity

One of the most fundamental requirements for doing good Theory – indeed one might say that if it's not obscure it's not Theory. It may be a theory, of course, but it's not Theory. Obscurity is essential, it's vital, it's of the essence; without it we're nothing. Writing that's clear and explicit and precise, that makes a logical argument that anyone can follow, that in fact makes any kind of argument or even positive statement at all as opposed to just throat-clearing and base-touching and genuflecting in a serpentine and inconclusive manner for X number of pages – that kind of writing is the enemy. In fact in a very real sense it may be the most dangerous enemy of all. Clarity, coherence, specificity, accessibility, and certainly elegance, aesthetic appeal, what's thought of as 'good writing' (see CANON), those are all just instruments of HEGEMONY. Obscurity is the opposite of all that. Obscurity is revolutionary, it's counter-hegemonic, it's TRANSGRESSIVE. It explodes the repressive bourgeois categories of LOGIC and REASON and POSITIVISM. So in solidarity with all the oppressed masses of the world, in the name of the Third World peoples and Muslims and women and pets we have to make our theoretical work as difficult to read and make sense of as possible.

Obsessive
What people are who are always talking about the NAZI connections of people like HEIDEGGER and de MAN; people who just can't let anything go and move on. Not of course to be used of Theorists who can't let anything go and move on.

Obsolete
Semi-criminal state of being. See FASHION.

Occupational hazards
Dehydration, skin allergies (via overexposure to chalk dust, tannic acid, wool), hypertrophy of vocal cords, myopia, monoculism, atypical gluteal morphology, libido admirationis, asomatic hearing deficit, speech-cessation impairment, preening behaviours, auto-inflation.

Oedipus complex
Well of course he was. We all are.

Oestrogen
Vitamin which creates different (and better) way of knowing, harmony, peace, silky-smooth skin, crocheting, and insistence on having toilet paper on the special roller-installation instead of sitting on sink.

Olympic Games

Horrible androcentric idea. Just a lot of testosterone driven men and women competing against each other. And all that flag-waving and national pride is just too much to bear. The SYNCHRONISED SWIMMING is good, though.

One

A beautiful number, all about unity, and wholeness, and holisticity, and simplicity. Plus it's so easy to count. But on the other hand a rather difficult number because not about diversity. Can be quite tricky to choose, actually, between DIVERSITY and HOLISM. Both are so good, and so admirable, yet they seem to contradict one another. That is very odd.

Opinion

Everything. Often confused, by pre-postmodern people, with entities like truth, reality, the world. 'That's just your opinion,' is the approved rebuke in such cases.

Opinion polling

Rigorous method for finding out what a population thinks when they think the same as we do. Hopelessly flawed mechanism for finding out only what you want to find out when they don't. See PSEPHOLOGY.

Opposites

Things to be reconciled, or better yet denied and ridiculed under the name 'binary opposition.' This is useful when people claim you are wrong about something.

Organic intellectual

Gramscian term for intellectual who never wears polyester or acrylic, though Gore-tex is allowed.

Orientalism

A discourse about the East (East of the West, obviously) that legitimated and enabled imperialism and colonialism, and that still to this very day allows Western writers to assume the paternalist privileges of the pukka sahib. Any old Smith or Jones can just pick up a pen and write essentialist discourse about people in India or someplace else in the East. Movies, too. It's odd that it never works the other way – that Indian or Egyptian writers, for instance, never make essentialist or Occidentalist statements about people in the US or UK. But so it is. There is obviously a very basic difference in the nature of the two peoples.

Orientation, sexual

Not to be confused with Orientalism.

Oslo

Eccentric Scandinavian city of no significance. Not a physicists' hangout, not a quantum city. See COPENHAGEN, STOCKHOLM.

Ossian

Gaelic bard from many centuries ago (his dates are uncertain) who wrote an epic about Gaelic hero Fingal. The poet James Macpherson published a newly edited version in 1760 to much acclaim. Cynical Tory pedants like Hume and Johnson said it was a fraud, because whenever anyone wanted to see the manuscript Macpherson had just that moment lent it to a friend in Cornwall or Tuscany. But of course it wasn't a fraud at all, Hume and Johnson were just jealous.

Paleo-Indians
Probably didn't arrive on the North American continent some 14,000 years ago. And if they did, they certainly didn't slaughter the whole woolly mammoth population, because they loved animals, and nature, and they ate berries instead, and kept the mammoths as pets. But not in captivity, obviously, because that would have been wrong.

Paradigm
A thing that shifts, thus proving that scientists merely make up their findings. See KUHN.

Paradoxical
Very much a word to be performed. Best used by people with thorough-going eyebrow independence. So, for example, if a pedantic philosopher complains that your claim that truth is relative to discourse appears to be self-defeating, raise just one eyebrow and say, 'Yes, it does seem to be somewhat paradoxical.' For maximum effect keep eyebrow raised for at least a minute. See EPISTEMOLOGY.

Paranoid-Schizoid position
Being terribly worried that people think you have a mental illness, which clearly is just mad.

Paris
1) The epicentre of EUROCENTRISM. Could be London, because of the empire, and analytical philosophy, and so on – but London is too far north, plus on an island which is, only doubtfully, real Europe. But nowhere else will do either.

81

Berlin is too far east (and too odd), Rome too far south (and has the Pope in it), Vienna too far east and south, etc. It has to be Paris. And that seems right, Paris has always been the European city.

2) The epicentre of Theory, postmodernism, deconstruction. Where all the biggies were or are – LACAN, Deleuze and Guattari, FOUCAULT, Kristeva, Irigaray, DERRIDA. Nirvana, Valhalla, the City on a Hill. Quite paradoxical considering (1), but then paradox is a very Paris thing.

Pavlov, Ivan
Russian physiologist who found that dogs tend to salivate when they hear a bell or come across a meringue shell filled with cream and fruit. See BEHAVIOURISM.

Peace
A beautiful thing, of course. See MENDEL.

Peasant farmer
Salt of the earth type who enjoys a harmonious relationship with Nature. Not too keen on the rain forest admittedly, but greatly fond of goats and colourful, as opposed to mono, crops. As a sworn enemy of global agribusiness, you won't catch a peasant farmer eating Rice Krispies or Weetabix unless he's really hungry or it's breakfast time. It is not true that peasant farmers tend to shoot anything that moves in their fields.

Pedestrian
1) (*n*.) Irritating life form that gets in the way and slows everything down. Wastes fuel because cars often have to slow down or even stop when pedestrians are crossing the street.
2) (*adj*.) Old hat, *vieux jeu*, unhip, like admiring Leavis or Shakespeare or some old bore like that.

Penis envy
It used to explain everything. Now it's patrolling borders that explains everything.

Peppered moth
1) Proved evolution false because someone found a black one on a speckled wall, or a speckled one on a black wall.
2) Delicious with a little garlic and parsley.

Permanent intercourse
According to KLEIN, a product of the primal scene. The child imagines the parents are locked in permanent intercourse, thus forming a single being of horrible strength and ingenuity, bent on terrorising and dominating the child and forcing it to stop chewing with its mouth open.

Perspective
Everybody has one, therefore nothing that anyone says is true. Or false. Except of course what I just said – that is true, but it is the only thing that is true. Or is there maybe one other thing … no, no, that's the only one.

Petri dish
Strange deformed little bowls in which scientists grow cultures. Not to be confused with real cultures, the important kinds.

Phallogocentric
Brilliant portmanteau word which points out that language is a profoundly male invention that excludes the female; therefore women ought not to use it, but just flap their hands and throw water around, instead. Phallogocentric DISCOURSE is linear and ego-oriented and used for the masculine languages of SCIENCE, philosophy, and high art, while women's discourse is less

structured and more communal, and used for the female languages of cooking, SWIMMING and religion.

Pharmaceuticals
Chemical compounds fed or injected into people to make them conform to normative ideas of health.

Phenomenal world
The world as it appears to the senses. Except, of course, if you're drunk or suffer from synaethesia. See NOUMENAL WORLD.

Phenotype
The important bit. Quite independent of the genotype. See GENES.

Philistine
Adjective to characterise people who fail to appreciate the mathematical argumentation of LACAN, the insights of FOUCAULT, the sheer unparalleled intelligence of Judith BUTLER, the performativity of Deleuze and Guattari.

Physics
A very male kind of science, all mathematics-driven and cold, all about taking things apart and staring at the pieces. Haunt of rude abusive sarcastic people like SOKAL. Easy; what people do who aren't smart enough to do Theory. See MATHEMATICS.

Placebo
Drug administered to the deceased during the Roman Catholic vespers for the dead. Doesn't tend to work, which pleases nobody, except maybe the Lord. See EXPERIMENT.

Plath, Sylvia
Poet; great role-model for women because she committed suicide.

Plato
Greek philosopher, educated in Egypt. In fact, he found most of his ideas buried under the pyramids and the Sphinx. There is absolutely no evidence for this claim, but that's one of the good things about Afrocentric history, evidence doesn't count. See ARISTOTLE, SOCRATES.

Pleasure principle
Person in charge of a particularly hip and happening institution of higher education. However, it is important to remember if you are such a person that you must never greet a student for a one-to-one session with the words, 'Hi there, I am the pleasure principle.'

Polyphemus
A favoured role model from Ancient Greece. Had an eye for the ladies. See HOMER.

Popper, Karl
Probably racist philosopher who suggested that what was important about SWANS was their colour. His antipathy towards swans of colour is said to have resulted from an early childhood mishap when he was savaged by his favourite pet, a black swan called Ludwig. Happily the claim that Ludwig was wielding a poker at the time has recently been falsified.

Popular culture
Culture created by sturdy workers and peasants in Hollywood and New York and London: movie producers, studio heads, record executives, owners of TV and radio stations, people like that. None of your arrogant snobbish elitist over-educated artsy-fartsy bookish

intellectuals who are out of touch with the people, no, the millionaires and billionaires who create popular culture are all good Tom Joads and Norma Raes every one of them.

Popular science
Yeah, right; oxymoron.

Positional goods
Goods whose value and desirability depends wholly or in part on the fact that other people don't have them. For example, a large office, no eight o'clock classes, no nine o'clock classes, no ten o'clock classes, no administrative duties, students who get crushes on one, being called a superstar in the national press, MANOLO BLAHNIK shoes.

Positivism
The insane, harmful, elitist idea that one should have some evidence before deciding something is true (see EMPIRICISM).

Postcolonialism
Theory and discipline dating from the late 1980s, inspired by the observation that Salman Rushdie had become quite famous, so scholars might as well exploit the fact. Thus the influential anthology *The Empire Writes Back* was named after an article by Rushdie. This prescient tactic was gloriously vindicated in the same year when Rushdie became a lot more famous because of the *fatwa*, which could be seen as a very postcolonialist and ironic way to become a star.

Postmodernism
At the pinnacle of hip disciplines and theory. Suspects and problematises all hierarchies, totalisations, grand narratives, universalisms, ideas of 'progress' and 'enlightenment.' A huge advance on

previous ways of thinking, brilliant at demystifying the dominant normativity of LOGOCENTRIC discourse. Everyone is slightly nervous about what's going to happen when Postpostmodernism comes along – but maybe it will just be exactly the same thing only more so.

Poststructuralism

Naturally: the minute everyone got the point about structuralism, DERRIDA interrupted with a critique of it and everyone had to start all over. Poststructuralism is often confused with POSTMODERNISM and DECONSTRUCTION, but this is a terrible mistake, because.

Prague

Quite good city. In central Europe, so escapes the worst taint of EUROCENTRISM; that is to say, not as Eurocentric as more marginal cities. (Which is slightly odd, since ordinarily it's the margin that's good and the centre that's bad – but probably this is just a case of deceptive nomenclature: actually Prague is on the margin and it's the places further west that are truly central; one just has to move the compass. See LOCATION.) In central Europe; generally considered quite bohemian; and the hometown of KAFKA, which makes it pretty hip.

Premature expostulation

Frequent cause of embarrassment during conference season. Academics, when listening to conference papers, excited by the presence of a wholly new CAPTIVE AUDIENCE, are often quite unable to contain themselves. At the most inopportune moments, usually when it's lunch time, they can't help but expostulate. And, by God, don't their expostulations go on for ever. The lesson to be learnt here is that if it's not you at the podium, even if you are the edgiest of edgy Theorists, the chances are nobody is interested in what you have to say. So don't say it.

Primatology
Study of high ranking bishops. Early primatologists found that their subjects were characterised by a superior development of hands and feet, a shortened snout, and a large brain. Modern primatologists, however, have questioned the large brain findings. Primate behaviour remains a source of fascination. They enjoy fancy dress, incense, sermonising and young children. They're not so keen on atheists, Sunday morning lie-ins or homosexuality. They're an endangered species in the United Kingdom, but thrive in less cynical environments.

Prison
Like hospitals and clinics in being places where people are punished, but the food is slightly better.

Progress
There are many possible forms of progress. You can be walking up (or down) a hill, and if someone asks you (by cell phone perhaps) how it's going, you can say you're making progress. But there could be a murderer at the top of the hill, or a tiger, or a blizzard. You can make progress and 'succeed' at reaching your 'goal' and still wind up with something not much good. So with science. There are many – perhaps infinite – ways it could make progress. Some might be good (useful, helpful, etc.) and some not. Some might get at the 'truth' and some might not. So science is not reliable.

Project
It's good to call everything a project. The ENLIGHTENMENT, humanism, NEW CRITICISM, NEW HISTORICISM, POSTMODERNISM – all projects. For things that are under suspicion, this conveys the idea of some sinister agenda; for things that are approved, it sounds dynamic and active and butch.

Proletariat

Salt of the earth types, they represent the liberatory potential of mankind, if only they would realise it. Attitude surveys suggest that some members of the proletariat – well, lots really – are disturbingly illiberal in their views. Happily, if they are, it is only because they live alienated lives. It's not because they're bastards. And, rest assured, as soon as the means of production are collectively owned, they'll turn into little angels. Even if they do end up squabbling over who has the biggest halo. See CLASS IN-ITSELF.

Proust, Marcel

French novelist. Quite good – gay, and pretty damn obvious about it for his time. Also asthmatic, reclusive, bedridden; so all in all, well worth a look.

Psephology

The study of why people will insist on voting the wrong way.

Psychiatry

Discipline which through its commitment to a medical model of mental illness seeks to pathologise creativity and imagination. It fails to recognise that people hear voices and think they're Jesus because of problems in the family. If only parents would stop involving children in their arguments over the television remote control, then the world would be a happier place. Anyway, the work of Rosenhan proved that most people in psychiatric hospitals are actually sane. The loonies are the psychiatrists. See ILLNESS, MEDICINE.

Psychic pressure

An inner force, similar to steam but not quite so damp, that fuels drives, for example, the SCOPIC DRIVE, the sex drive, the AGORIC DRIVE.

Psychopathology

A discursive form which constitutes the category 'mental illness' as an object of knowledge, generates criteria by which to distinguish mental illness from its binary opposite, and generates strategies for the treatment of this 'illness'. It's obvious what an intrusive, colonising project this is, and how unjust it is to deprive people of their mental 'illness' when they so desperately long to hang on to it.

Public intellectual

Dangerous phenomenon. Cuts into respect and admiration owed to academics. See BOTTON.

Punctuated equilibrium

Idea developed by Stephen Jay Gould and some other less famous bloke which suggests that evolution spends most of its time doing not very much at all. This is just as it should be. See SOCIOBIOLOGY.

Quantum

First name of various ideas that no one understands, least of all scientists, so it makes a great METAPHOR for chaos, complexity, RELATIVITY, randomness, POSTMODERNITY, and just about anything one needs a metaphor for.

Quark

A kind of soft cheese – German I think, or perhaps Swedish. Serve in tiny portions.

Quasar
Places far away where really bad DJs are banished.

Quasi-algebraic formulae
Polite term for what others denominate pseudo-algebraic formulae in the work of LACAN, who liked to re-write some of his assertions in algebraic-looking form (letters, horizontal lines, etc) that in mathematical terms meant strictly nothing at all. See CONVENTIONAL MATHEMATICS.

Quibble
What people are doing when they say I'm wrong about something. Not to be used when *I* say people are wrong about something. See NITPICKING.

Quixote, Don
A hero, he fought a giant suspected of biological determinism.

Rampage
Very butch MALE Theorists don't so much INTERROGATE texts, as rampage all over them. Hence if you listen carefully during coffee breaks at the MODERN LANGUAGE ASSOCIATION CONVENTION, you'll hear people saying things like 'I rampaged all over Molly Bloom last night' and 'I gave those rabbits in *Watership Down* a right rampaging'. See DEAD RABBITS.

Rand, Ayn
Hollywood screenwriter, later writer of huge thick novels, then a philosopher, but for some reason I can never find her in the

philosophy reference books I look in. Maybe I have the spelling wrong.

Random access memory
Memory disorder linked to PREMATURE EXPOSTULATION. You're sitting through a boring conference paper on transgendered giraffes when suddenly it pops into your head that you haven't fed your pet snake her daily guinea pig. At this point, it is very important not to let out a cry of 'My snake needs her guinea', especially if you're at a conference organised by some vegetarian pressure group. The best cure for such inconvenient memory tricks is to snooze through conference papers.

Rape
What scientists do to Nature, Mother Earth, Gaia, Oil-seeds. See BACON, NEWTON.

Rape manual
Newton's *Principia*.

Readers' liberation
Movement that began in the 1970s after the Stone Hall riot (May 1971) when a group of oppressed readers took to the streets to protest the narrow univocal interpretation of Trollope's *The Small House at Allington* that F. R. Leavis had forced on them in his text *The Great Tradition and Don't You Forget It*. After three days of marching back and forth between Columbia and Harlem (getting 'down' with the brothers and sisters *en route*), the readers won the right to view the small house as a sign for the female genitalia if they really wanted to. They were also permitted to do the same with selected Laura Ingalls Wilder texts provided they waited until 9 p.m.

Realism

The naive view that there is a fact of the matter about the world and it is possible to get at it. Some mathematician guy called Alfred Tarski has something to do with this view. He claimed the sentence 'Snow is white' is true, if and only if, snow is white. At first sight one might think that he had too much time on his hands when he came up with this. But then one realises it isn't actually right. The reason has to do with the SORITES PARADOX. This shows that snow can be simultaneously white and not-white. Which means that 'Snow is white' can be true, even if snow isn't white. Can't philosophy be exhilarating when done well! Anyway, what this adds up to is that there is no fact of the matter about the world, and snow is sometimes white and sometimes not. This means realism is false. See BIVALENCE.

Reality check

Fashion item. 'I wore my new reality check shirt at the curriculum committee meeting today and everyone said I looked quasi-presentable.'

Reason

Bad, toxic entity, that foolish people use when they ought to use their inner voice, or angels, or INTUITION, or a gut feeling, or their hearts, or the *I Ching*.

Reductionism

Reducing something we like to something we don't (genes primarily).

Regard, le

The look or the gaze. SARTRE, LACAN, and FOUCAULT all worried a great deal about the gaze, but they needn't have bothered. What they failed to realise of course is that when people seem to be staring at oneself, they are actually thinking about their own dinner or sex life or new shoes.

Reichian therapy

Based on a simple idea. If a person has a head cold, with a blocked nose, then probably they feel a tad irritated. Similarly, if a person's vital energies, their life-source, if you like, are blocked, then more than likely they're not going to be best pleased. The solution is to unblock the blockage, and let the energy flow. This is a bit like bleeding a radiator only without the little key. It also involves orgasms – another sense in which it is unlike most plumbing – since these are a great source of relaxation, especially if accompanied by a cigarette afterwards. Evidence for the efficacy of Reichian therapy is found amongst the BONOBOS. Orgasms take up between 30 and 40 percent of their waking hours, and you'll never find a bonobo in a psychiatric ward.

Reification

Mental process by which, under late CAPITALISM, everything begins to resemble canned goods (see COMMODITY FETISHISM). Under very late capitalism everything begins to resemble a DVD player.

Relations of production

The family of the tools and raw materials of production. See MEANS OF PRODUCTION.

Relative zero

1)   Any temperature around –270 to –250° centigrade – an approximate ABSOLUTE ZERO.
2)   That tiresome geeky cousin of yours who is no good at parties.

Relativity

What Einstein had a very special theory of, which means that it's all, like, relative.

Religion

1) Organised religion not all that good because oppressive and, frankly, organised, except of course when it's other people's organised religion, in the Third World and so on, and Third World people in the First World. But apart from that, spirituality is better than religion, although in a very real sense it's all the same thing in the end, and we are all One.

2) Another word for science.

Replicability

Supposedly a technique for establishing the truth of a hypothesis, it is actually a job creation scheme for scientists. If they were capable of original thought, they'd be Theorists. They're not, as evidenced by the fact that they all wear the same style white coat, so they spend their time repeating each other's experiments.

Repressive

A feature of things like REASON, LINEAR THINKING, LOGIC and other forms of patriarchal, hegemonic, PHALLOGOCENTRIC discourse. Not liberatory. 'Like postmodern social theory, postmodern science sees modernity and modern reason as inherently repressive.' (Steven Best, 'Chaos and Entropy: Metaphors in Postmodern Science and Social Theory')

Repressive desublimation

Freud and Marx in one phrase, it's positively arousing. Arousal must be quickly redirected though, because repressive desublimation is bad. Pretty much it means that rather than being sexually excited by experimental texts people are sexually excited by fast cars and DVD players. As a result, they forget to rebel and CAPITALISM continues on its merry way. The hippies tried to do something about this sorry state of affairs, but they were too lazy to rebel in quite the right kind of way, and then they got well-paid jobs, fast cars and DVD players, and that was that. A bit of a downer really.

Repressive tolerance

MARCUSIAN term for 'you just can't win.' Well, it's typical, isn't it. You no sooner get through explaining how the BOURGEOISIE manages everything and represses the hell out of all of us when what does it do, it says 'No we don't, you can do anything you want to, go ahead. Take all your clothes off, make fun of us, grope each other in public, scribble obscenities, we don't care.' So now what do we do? What can we do but decide that's the most repressive move of all and ask Marcuse to give it a name for us.

Resisting reader

One who reads against the grain of the text, who calls its meaning into question, and who considers this activity inherently political. No matter how the forces of dominant narrativity try to bend the RR to their will, the brave Reader will not give in. So the RR reads *Harry Potter and the Goblet of Fire* as a Russian play about bored provincials in Oklahoma, *Discipline and Punish* as a poem about the low carbohydrate diet, and *The Dialectic of Enlightenment* as a newspaper article about the shortage of tennis socks in rural Nigeria. As a result all the institutions, paradigms, normativities, discourses, hegemonies and projects of late CAPITALISM tremble, sway back and forth, and collapse in a heap.

Return of the repressed

If the repressed is too big or too small or the wrong colour or doesn't go with those shoes, it can be returned for a partial refund. See MANOLO BLAHNIK.

Roswell

Fun place in New Mexico desert where something fell down in 1947. It's not clear what the something was. POSITIVISTS and bureaucrats and the Feds say it was a weather balloon. UFOlogists say it was an extraterrestrial vehicle with aliens aboard, and that there are photographs of the alien autopsies. The latter seems far-fetched, but the work of John MACK at Harvard is – well, interesting, anyway. And nobody can prove the something was not an alien vehicle, so there is really no reason not to think it was. See FAIRIES AT THE BOTTOM OF THE GARDEN.

Rousseau, Jean-Jacques
So much nicer than that awful Bacon, even though he did hand all his children over to an orphanage because he couldn't be bothered. At least he didn't want to rape Nature.

Royalty
1) The author's percentage.
2) Dynastic system that produces experts on architecture, complementary medicine, horses, corgis, fast cars, wild life preservation, hunting, etc.

Sadism
Propensity discovered by FOUCAULT, drawing on the work of FREUD, NIETZSCHE and the Marquis de Sade, for humans to enjoy inflicting pain on one another and when that's not available on animals. Odd that no one noticed before Foucault.

Samoa
The place to come of age.

Sartre, Jean-Paul
Exemplary philosopher of freedom. Showed how the FRUIT FLY is in ANGUISH, when confronted by the inevitability of its freedom; and how it employs strategies of bad faith – pretending to be human,

for example – in a desperate attempt to avoid the compulsion to choose freely.

Saussure, Ferdinand de
Linguist whose work undermined the idea that propositions acquire their truth-value by picking out real objects or states of affair in the world. It is now thought that his surname is a *nom de plume* which became established in his undergraduate years as a result of his tendency to ask people how they could be so sure that a word meant what they thought it meant.

Schizophrenia
A different way of seeing the world. Invented by Thomas Szasz.

Schrödinger's cat
Half alive; half undead. A vampire moggy.

Science
1) An inconvenient discipline that tends to undermine our most cherished beliefs.
2) A tiny cabal of powerful people who ignore what the majority of humanity believe.
3) A civil religion.
4) Part of the ideological state apparatus. Science 'like the Church before it, is a supremely social institution, reflecting and reinforcing the dominant values and views of society at each historical epoch.' (Richard Lewontin, *Biology as Ideology*)

Science fiction
Well of course it is.

Scientist

1) Wicked, elitist, narrow-minded member of tiny unelected aristocracy which does not share the beliefs of the great majority of people. Andrew Ross writes in *Strange Weather*: 'How can metaphysical life (New Age) theories and explanations taken seriously by millions be ignored or excluded by a small group of powerful people called 'scientists'?'

2) A bourgeois, legitimator of capitalist exploitation. As Lewontin, Kamin and Rose said in *Not in our Genes*: 'Science is the ultimate legitimator of bourgeois ideology.' See STARBUCKS.

3) A dull, plodding, unimaginative person who only knows how to count things; a bore; a geek, a nerd, a swot, a grind.

Scopic drive

Psychic pressure to stare or gaze at people, especially for men to gaze at women, especially in movies. Some Theorists interpret this drive as part of a move to dominate and control, others think it may possibly have something to do with the sex drive. A sublimated form of this drive is thought to explain the compulsive attraction of scientists to TELESCOPES and MICROSCOPES. The idea originates with LACAN; Martha Marinara says this about it in 'Death, Domesticity, and the Feminine Gaze': 'For Lacan, the gaze is always an act of desired appropriation: "We can apprehend this privilege of the gaze in the function of desire". Seeing becomes desire – part of the scopic drive in which the eye functions as a phallus.' See AGORIC DRIVE, SUDORIC DRIVE.

Sea Horse

Socially progressive animal which has subverted traditional gender roles by arranging it so that its males have babies. It's thought likely that they originated in Samoa. Their reputation as the world's most right-on animal was damaged recently when it emerged that they are monogamous. Should not be confused with actual horses.

Seems

A word to use where something really doesn't seem to be the case, but it would be unseemly to admit it. For example: 'It certainly seems like Luce Irigaray has a good point to make'; or 'Starbucks seems to be responsible for world starvation, George Bush and cappuccino'.

Self-esteem

What children go to school to learn. The curriculum.

Self-praise

A necessary activity, because no one else will do it, so Theorists have to say explicitly how brilliant they are. The phrase 'highly sophisticated theory' is useful for this.

Semiological opposition

Has to do with the way semiotics explains that words mean what they do by not meaning other things: so cat means cat because it doesn't mean bat or mat or car. Therefore if you're writing a story in which a cat sat on a mat and a rat and a bat in a hat sat in a car, you'd better pay close attention, and proof-read it several times.

Seven types of intelligence

Great invention or rather discovery of Howard Gardner that gets around the whole distressing matter of inequalities in intelligence among people. Because it turns out that there are seven of them, types of intelligence, where everyone had thought there was just one. 'ONE' can be a very good, spiritual word in the right context, but in the wrong context it's not; it's divisive and bad. Seven, on the other hand, is an almost magical number, as everyone knows. Seven deadly sins, Seven Types of Ambiguity, Seven Up, Seven-Eleven, Seven Crown, the Magnificent Seven, Seven Brides for Seven Brothers. So with seven to draw on, one person may be smart at mathematics and science, but another person is smart at fighting or poker or burglary or crying. So it all evens out.

Sexual metaphor
The method by which science achieved its otherwise inexplicable success. Bacon's talk about scientists raping nature got a lot of men excited about doing science (and nature) in the seventeenth century, and that's how science got started. Otherwise it never would have, people would have stuck to dear alchemy and magic instead and everything would have been much better.

Shopping mall
Where it all comes together. Discipline, normativity, repressive sublimation – it's not as if you can take all your clothes off there, or run around with a dead rabbit on your head squealing and singing 'The Internationale,' is it? CONSUMERISM, COMMODITY FETISHISM – what else are you there for? Science and technology – somebody plugged everything in and made the cash registers work, right? MARX, FREUD, POSTMODERNISM – money and sex get together and wipe out truth, so we might as well go shopping.

Sidestep
A manoeuvre to make a virtue of when you don't know how to answer an objection. Donna Haraway explained how it works in this interview in *Socialist Review* 21, no. 2: 'Plainly the social constructivist argument has its limitations, because it ends in relativism... I find that the most enlivening philosophical work tries to sidestep that set of philosophical traps...'

Significant
Adjective to use of work that you suspect is not well-founded or even sane, but is by someone on your side.

Situated
Everyone is situated, because everyone is somewhere, no one is nowhere. Therefore there is no Truth because what is true over there is not true back here, and vice versa.

Slide of the signifier

The signifier always slides under the signified (or possibly it's the other way around). This can be written mathematically, and was, by LACAN: S/s This may seem too banal to be worth mentioning but it's not, it's so profound that it explains everything. That's why literary theorists are central to every discipline, and why they're equipped to tell philosophers, historians, physicists, neuroscientists and everyone else what's what.

Snappiest dressers

Literary theorists.

Sneeze

A highly abbreviated orgasm confined to the nose and sinus cavity. This geographic fact caused FREUD to think nasal surgery could cure certain neuroses. It was a shrewd guess but turned out to be not quite correct. The piece of gauze was a mistake but Freud did apologise, or at least admit it happened, so enough already.

Social control

As FOUCAULT discovered, SCIENCE and REASON have been used ever since the ENLIGHTENMENT to control everyone, via hospitals, prisons, asylums, schools, roads, railways, maps, schedules, clocks, accounting, tax returns, measuring spoons, traffic lights, and lined paper. All this completely rules out human spontaneity, creativity, originality, fantasy, play, fun, pleasure, sex, authenticity, freedom, libido and aggression. Thus science and reason are obviously terrible things and should be abandoned forthwith in favour of the free play and carnival and licence of the Middle Ages.

Social phenomenon

Science is a social phenomenon. No one bothers to deny this. Science is almost never done by single individuals who have no contact with other humans. It wouldn't amount to much without laboratories, conferences, plumbing supply shops. Therefore its findings are social, therefore they are contingent. That means that in some other social context they would be different. Therefore they are unreliable.

Social Text

A brilliant theoretical journal which did not deserve the childish practical joke that SOKAL played on it. If it even was a joke. There are those who think Sokal meant every hokey word but then pretended it was a joke when one of his physicist friends told him it was gibberish. In which case he lacks the courage it takes to be a Theorist. If it was a joke, then it's a violation of the absolute standards of scholarly discourse. Scholars are supposed to trust each other. If researchers say they've found a way to get cold fusion, or a cure for flu, or evidence that the data of science are not written in nature, one is supposed to trust them, not go poking around with a MICROSCOPE testing every little thing. Scholars are not cops or the Border Patrol. But jealous threatened scientists think they need to police their borders all the time, making sure all those edgy scary radicals from the Theory Department aren't getting over the fence and making trouble in their cosy little white male world.

Sociobiology

Absurd, probably NAZI-like, idea that social behaviour can be explained in evolutionary terms. However, in this instance, unlike in the case of DE MAN, its connection with National Socialist ideology cannot be excused. The nature of this connection isn't precisely clear – though it probably has something to do with EUGENICS – but, even so, it isn't worth taking any chances. Therefore, the best policy is simply to throw water at anybody who suggests that evolution has anything to do with social behaviour. After all, we haven't evolved as thinking, cooperative beings to tolerate this kind of Darwinist nonsense.

Sociology

There are quite a few good things about sociology. It can be quite trendy. There are French sociologists. Sociology students tend to look like Che Guevara. It isn't a science (no, really, it isn't). But it has dark secrets. Auguste Comte, all dignity and splendour, for one. He wanted to introduce a science of society, of all things. He was absolutely positive about that. And he also said that society progresses, which, to be frank, is the kind of claim which belongs in the dark ages. And then there's the fact that sociology has a methodology. That's okay when it is methodology beyond methodology. But when it involves things like counting and statistics it's a methodology too far. So sociology is good and bad. Light and dark. A bit like chocolate. See CHI-CHI.

Socrates

A famous African philosopher.

Socratic deformation

Elenchusitis. A psychic bend or swelling caused by spending many hours a day in a top-down interaction with people who are younger, more ignorant and usually (however temporarily) much sillier than oneself. Initial stages involve slight inflation of ego and a louder voice, intermediate stage causes sharp diminution in how long one can wait before interrupting anyone else who is talking, and terminal stage manifests complete inability to hear conflicting opinions, delusions of infallibility, grandiosity and monologuing behaviour, and chronic sustained hallucinations.

Sokal, Alan

1) A bad man, who tricked the brilliant, POSTMODERN journal, *Social Text*, into publishing a spoof article, and then told the world about it. The world thought it was funny, which just goes to show that it wasn't.

2) Adjective to use in front of silly words, as in 'sokalled reason', 'sokalled science', 'sokalled evidence'.

Solid
A male thing. Not female. Obviously. See FLUID.

Sorites paradox
The view that bald people can be simultaneously bald and not-bald, and that snow can be simultaneously white and not-white. It is necessary to be able to subtract in order to understand this paradox. See REALISM.

Soul
Well, not exactly sure, sort of an outdated idea really, but it's kind of unspiritual to say so, and anyway it refers to something, though I don't exactly know what. Kind of the part of us that POSITIVISTS and SCIENTISTS and REDUCTIONISTS and people like that leave out, the part that can't be measured and is a little mysterious.

Species being
Idea developed by Karl MARX, based on an original theme by HEGEL. Pretty much it means that human beings freely engage in social production and consumption. And in doing so they externalise their nature in the world and in social relations. This sounds like poppycock. But it's a nice idea, anyway. It's got to be good to cooperate, for example. And we all understand the sense of pride which comes from the production of a new experimental text. But it does seem a bit essentialist about human nature. Perhaps a watered down version would be better? How about that human beings like to visit DIY stores on a Sunday, and occasionally put up shelves in their houses, though often they don't have the right number of screws. That's more like it. See ALIENATION, PROLETARIAT.

Spiritual

What to call a belief that perhaps is not terribly plausible or even possible but makes people feel special and magical.

Standard deviation

Statistical measure of innovation in an experimental text. One standard deviation is pretty good going. Should at least get you an invitation to the MLA Convention; the *Maryland Library Association* Convention, that is, not the MODERN LANGUAGE ASSOCIATION CONVENTION. You'll need two standard deviations for that.

Starbucks

A place where scientists drink coffee.

Stockholm

Dangerous city for an EDGY, urban, POSTMODERN Theorist to live. The trouble is that if you make Stockholm your home you're likely to go over to the other side (see DE MAN). Instead of producing radical, TRANSGRESSIVE theories, you'll probably find yourself working in a lab, counting things and worrying about REPLICABILITY. This effect is thought to be the result of Stockholm's proximity to COPENHAGEN, the famous quantum city.

Stonehenge

Large stone erection or megalith built by Celts or Druids to tell the time, keep track of the seasons, worship the sun, measure things, do magic, liven up Salisbury Plain, and for exercise. Was a very magical place when built and has become more and more so over the years. Absolutely full of magic now, also police, souvenir shops, tour buses, witches, wiccans, travellers, hippies, pseuds, ravers, ecstasy, journalists, academics, paranormal phenomena, investigators of paranormal phenomena. Fun place.

Story
What everything is, really, when you come right down to it.
Science, history, religion, mathematics, engineering – it's all a story.

Stove, David
Australian philosopher who proved beyond a shadow a doubt that
not every word Darwin wrote in the *Origin* turned out to be correct.
The word 'every' on page 66, for example, is decidedly dodgy. And
the word 'each' on page 78, isn't much better. He wrote a book
called *Darwinian Fairytales*. In light of recent misunderstandings, it
is important to note that Stove wasn't the one spinning the
fairytales. See MIDGLEY, QUIXOTE.

Strange attractors
Term from the science of chaos denoting people who fall into the
bottom quartile in terms of their ability to elicit a positive aesthetic
response, who nevertheless get lots of sex. Probably as a result of
fluctuations in their quantum chi fields or something. Also, they're
often rich and famous, which may not be a coincidence.

Straw man
Very useful prop for doing theory. Announce that pretheoretical
types believe in transcendent universals and the unquestioned
authority of straight white men and that Shakespeare never wrote
a bad line and other things that no one does believe or ever talk
about in such silly terms – and then declare your brave, defiant
opposition to all such hegemonic discourse, and everyone will be
overwhelmed by your daring rebellious stance and want to have
sex with you. See MIDGLEY, QUIXOTE, STOVE.

Strong programme

A dynamic aerobic (see LYOTARD) workout routine developed by the sociology department at the University of Edinburgh. Enables robust, muscle-bound, butch sociologists to dominate and frighten weak, timid, nerdy scientists.

Subversive performativity

BUTLERIAN term for activities such as women dressing up as Rambo or the Terminator or Dirty Harry or Calvin Coolidge and men dressing up as a Barbie doll or Marilyn Monroe or Margaret Thatcher or Mother Teresa.

Subvert

Verb not unlike transgress, deconstruct, undermine, problematise, put into question. Also, like them, in need to use caution: one must subvert other people's discourses and ideologies but never one's own.

Sudoric drive

Psychic pressure to sweat copiously. Explains otherwise baffling behaviour of people who run for miles or perform repetitive arduous pulling and lifting acts on a metal apparatus. See SCOPIC DRIVE.

Superstition

An elitist, intolerant word used by narrow-minded LINEAR THINKERS and POSITIVISTS for deeply spiritual beliefs held by billions of people.

Suspicion

Absence of suspicion is naive and pretheoretical. It is imperative to be suspicious of people's projects, their attempts to foreclose, the way their paradigms function to foreclose futures that cause anxiety. And always in a tone reeking of heavy innuendo and implication. 'We know what he's afraid of.' We don't, of course, but it's so useful to say we do.

Swan

Contrary creature. You count a thousand white swans, and then, wouldn't you know it, a black one comes along. This might be the same problem as afflicted the PEPPERED MOTH. See POPPER.

Synchronised swimming

An exemplary sport. Its synchronised aspects suggest HOLISM and thorough-going intersubjectivity. Its water-immersion aspects suggest birth and, therefore, new life and mothering. Its breath-holding aspects suggest discipline and self-denial. And all that leg-waving requires radical limb independence, which is suggestive of YOGA and Eastern religions. Best of all, you do get the occasional drowning, which adds a smidgen of excitement to the whole event. See HERACLITUS.

Taboo

Taboos cannot be universal, but they can be a good thing. They are especially good when they belong to indigenous peoples. Some taboos involve menstruation. This is unfortunate, but let's face it women can be a pain at that time of the month. Taboos are also good when they apply to things that we really ought not talk about. IQ and GENES, for example. Race and pretty much anything except affirmative action. Paul de MAN and the NAZIS. NIETZSCHE and the Nazis. HEIDEGGER and the Nazis. Hannah Arendt, Heidegger and the Nazis. DEEP ECOLOGY and the Nazis. Well pretty much anything to do with Nazis, really.

Telescope

An instrument that scientists use to look at things that are so big and far away that no one cares about them.

Television

Once thought to be an instrument of bourgeois HEGEMONY and CONSUMERISM, but now Theory has a more sophisticated understanding; it has discovered that TV is a site of resistance and an area of audience agency. This is good because it means TV is theorisable, which is to say theorists can write about TV shows instead of books, which means they can watch TV instead of reading, which is quicker, easier and more fun, plus it's easier to eat, floss your teeth, and have sex while doing it (though if you have sex you may need to rewind parts).

Testosterone

Poison which destroys intuition, warmth, niceness and gossip. Never mix with Y.

The Gene Genie

David Bowie song about pioneering genetic engineer.

Theodicy

Homeric tale of one man and his travails to defend the goodness of God. See HOMER, POLYPHEMUS.

Theory

What literary critics call literary criticism when they've read a few books, or at least an article or two, from other disciplines.

Therapeutic touch

Energy medicine which emerged in the nursing community in the United States. It doesn't involve any actual touching – after all, that would carry a risk of MRSA infection – but rather a wafting of the hands around the body. This apparently results in reinvigorated energy flows, which is excellent news if you've been suffering from one of the many REICHIAN blockage syndromes. Apparently it works because of CHI-CHI. So it's nice to know that that panda had a use after all.

Thermodynamics

Has a very important second law. Something to do with chaos, GÖDEL and QUANTUM things. To be invoked in order to demonstrate that nature always prefers disorder to order, as is demonstrated, for example, in post-war Iraq and most high-school classrooms. CREATIONISTS love the second law, which is odd because they aren't usually so keen on science. There are also first and third laws of thermodynamics, but they're not so important. And it is said that there is a 'zeroth' law, but that can't be true, 'zeroth' isn't a word. Thermodynamics is important even without its laws. For example, it explains hot air, roast MOA and the heat retaining properties of a yurt.

Thinking

A suspect and risky activity. The NAZIS had a saying: 'To think is already to doubt.' It's a shame it was the Nazis who said it, because it is so true.

Threatened

Adjective modifying people who fail to be impressed by the bold rebellious TRANSGRESSIVE ideas that I adhere to.

Thus

A useful word to insert between two arbitrary assertions, thus making both appear to be vaguely justified. Edward Said used it brilliantly in this sentence from *Orientalism*: 'Orientalism responded more to the culture that produced it than to its putative object, which was also produced by the West. Thus the history of Orientalism has both an internal consistency and a highly articulated set of relationships to the dominant culture surrounding it.'

Tobacco
Very dangerous if genetically modified.

Tolerance
Believing whatever I say, with no questions asked.

Topology
A kind of mathematics that deals with the way things look from very high places. Also called 'peak dynamics'.

Transference
Term from the psychoanalytic tradition describing the process whereby the analysand transfers all possessions to the analyst in order to pay for the therapy.

Transgressive
Dangerous, subversive, wicked. Border-violating, boundary-hopping, rule-breaking. A woman carrying a machine gun, a man wearing a hair-ribbon, a cat reading *Dogs Never Lie About Love*, a dog reading *Discipline and Punish*.

Trees
Should not be cut down, except to make way for new holiday homes in Tuscany or to provide paper for experimental texts.

Truth
A quaint, old-fashioned word, like bustle or barouche-landau or button-hook. No longer needed.

Tuscany
De rigueur holiday destination for the trendiest of literary theorists. Named after bits of Hannibal's elephants. Not Hannibal Lecter, he didn't have elephants.

Twin set
Woolly, sheep-derived fashion item worn by royalty. So good because woolly and fashion, but not so good because of sheep derivation, plus not actually all that fashionable, in fact not a bit fashionable except to royalty, and not all of them. The kind of royalty that shows up in *Hello* a lot never wears twin sets, while the kind that worries about wildlife while hunting wears them several times a day. Fashion can be confusing, as can royalty.

Twin studies
Necessarily flawed. See BURT.

Twins
The most important point is that zygosity has no part to play in understanding twins. Monozygotic and dizygotic twins are the same kinds of entities, and twin studies which show otherwise are probably fraudulent. Indeed, there really should be a campaign for the abolition of the word twin. Clearly, it objectifies in its designation of identity. People are unique, after all. Twins just aren't like that freaky DOLLY THE SHEEP. See IDENTICAL TWINS.

Uncertainty
Concept in physics. Means the calculations never come out right, which is why everything always misses. So nothing is true, which gives everyone a lot of leeway.

Uncompromising

Adjective to describe criticisms or rebukes or jeremiads by POSTMODERNISTS and right-on people. Not to be used of criticisms or rebukes or jeremiads by non-right-on people, by cultural conservatives and people like that, where adjectives like obtuse, offensive, ethnocentric, reactionary, geeky and so on are what's appropriate.

Undergraduates

A nuisance in many ways but good for the ego. See SELF-ESTEEM.

Universalism

A suspect category, an instrument of HEGEMONY, a relic of the ENLIGHTENMENT, a covert way of excluding the Other. Because what is labelled 'Universal' is often (always?) in fact male and/or European and/or bourgeois, straight, etc. So for instance the valorisation of REASON and LOGIC obviously excludes women. The privileging of justice, democracy, equal treatment before the law obviously excludes other cultures – billions of people, with their love of HIERARCHY and subordination, simply ignored; it's outrageous.

Universities

Factories for the production of capitalist ideology. As Lewontin, Kamin and Rose say in *Not in Our Genes*, 'Science is the ultimate legitimator of bourgeois ideology... If biological determinism is a weapon in the struggle between classes, then the universities are weapons factories, and their teaching and research faculties are the engineers, designers, and production workers.'

Venus of Willendorf
Deeply beautiful figure of woman with a faceless head and an enormous spherical abdomen, which shows that women used to rule the world.

Vienna
Interesting place. Source of good things and bad things. FREUD, good, but also LOGICAL POSITIVISM chapter two, bad.

Vienna Circle
Named after the Riesenrad, the famous giant ferris wheel that plays such a large part in *The Third Man*. The Vienna Circle was a group of philosophers, Carnap and so on, who were behind the second wave of LOGICAL POSITIVISM, the first being in the nineteenth century sometime.

Vieux jeu
French for stale news, last week.

Voice
Something women have a different one of.

Wage labour
New form of slavery, only with fewer chains and less rowing.

Wakefield

City in Yorkshire, UK known for textiles, dyestuff and high incidence of measles, mumps and rubella. See MMR.

Wales

Tiny endangered country that kind people work to save. Uphill battle due to unfortunate local monarch, the 'Prince' of Wales, famous polymath and medical advisor with eccentric passion for absorbent products. See CHARLES.

Wallace, Alfred Russel

Almost certainly, like DARWIN, a Stock Exchange dabbling economist, which explains how he independently hit upon the theory of evolution by natural selection. He is thought to have lost an 'l' from his middle name after an early childhood mutation mishap. Gave up economics for naturalism in the 1840s. Nudity on the Stock Exchange just wouldn't have been tolerated.

War of position

Gramscian notion describing the lengths which some people will go to in order to acquire POSITIONAL GOODS.

Weather forecasting

Very difficult, except in Saudi Arabia. Computer models of the weather are constantly undermined by the fact that the small numbers of genes of BUTTERFLIES means that they have free will. Consequently, they will insist on flapping their wings unpredictably. The result is chaos. You predict sunshine, and you get a tornado. You go for a tornado, and a hurricane turns up. The butterflies affect nonchalance, but it's obvious they're enjoying it. The bastards.

Weather, heavy

A good thing to make of quite basic, clear, elementary observations. As in: 'Language is not transparent, words change their meaning over time, it is necessary to be aware of this in order to think and talk clearly and precisely.' By making heavy weather of this truism one can spin it out indefinitely and create dissertations, articles, conference papers, books, anthologies and entire libraries. This phenomenon may be related to chaos (see WEATHER FORECASTING) and BUTTERFLIES in some real but difficult to pin down way. A Theorist taps a key in Paris and there is a hurricane of verbiage in New Haven and Durham and Brighton – something like that.

Werther, Young

Fictional character who, like Chatterton, set a fashion for suicide. See GOETHE.

Whales

Small, unpleasant country that no one wants to save. Too full of coal and blubber, and has horrible festival-type thing called Eistedfodd where people sing in incomprehensible clicks and groans, not like music at all, sounds like someone gargling under water.

Whiggish

A useful pejorative to indicate a fatuously optimistic portrayal of a subject one wants to attack. So a 'whiggish history of science' is one that mistakenly considers science a good thing.

Whitman, Walt

Poet. Very good because gay, and pretty blunt about it for his time. Also because free verse poet, so subversive of confining formalism of metre and rhyme. Slightly overenthusiastic patriot, but that's forgivable.

Wilde, Oscar

Good man. Closeted, of course, but still very TRANSGRESSIVE for the time, and got off a lot of brilliant jokes. Died in Paris.

Will to Believe

Something William James discovered, so we can all believe whatever we want to, and you can't stop us.

Wisdom

1) What people have naturally, that gets knocked out of them by school, rules, right angles, scales, graph paper, maps, meters, decimal systems and zippers. Wisdom isn't the same as intelligence or knowledge, of course; in fact it's sort of the opposite. It's especially the opposite of mathematics and science. Maths is about numbers, which is about counting. You can only count things – stamps, coins, bullets, nails, genes. Wisdom is about the things you can't count – love, and beauty, and the spirit, and soup.

2) A kind of tooth.

Woolly thinking

The opposite of linear, ratiocentric thinking. So it must be good. The expression probably derives from the sartorial elegance of the cutting edge Theory lecturers of the 1980s. Wool was *de rigueur*, and all was right in the academy. Heady days.

X

The source of special knowledge, intuition, warmth, niceness and gossip.

X-Files, the

Brilliant paranoid television show that explored (possibly METAPHORICALLY) the many concealments and lies of the US government. The two protagonists were FBI agents, one a sceptical rationalist, the other a believer in every possible supernatural entity and occurrence. As in real life, every week the sceptic had it wrong and the believer had it right. Neither one of them ever cracked a smile for the entire run of the show – it was serious stuff.

Y

The source of LOGIC, LINEAR THINKING, analysis, football, war, and not talking about Feelings; probably a mistake.

Yoga

Famous bear from Jellystone Park. He is renowned for his breathing control, his ability to get his limbs into ridiculous positions and his tendency to irritate park rangers. It is very important to realise that bears are not wild animals, but rather kind, considerate, chilled-out pets. See BI-POLAR DISORDER.

Zarathustra

A super man.

Zeitgeist

Something it is everyone's first duty to be in touch with. See FASHION, EDGE.

Zen

The best way to do most things. Just kind of like let it happen, man.

Zenophobia

Irrational dislike of motorbike riding Buddhists. See ZEN.

Zeus

Testosterone-soaked sky god who had a problem with monogamy.

Zoology

The branch of sociology devoted to the study of zoos. Currently, the discipline is largely characterised by a rather unfortunate empirical methodology. Basically, zoologists spend their time counting things – penguins, for example. It was different in the past. Old-style zoologists were diverted by intractable and esoteric questions. Such as: Why bother with lions in zoos when they're always fast asleep behind the biggest clump of grass for a thousand miles? And: What's the point of the giant panda (see CHI-CHI)? Unfortunately, old-style zoology didn't survive the empirical turn, and is now as dead as the Moa. But happily there is a new kid on the block to challenge the hegemony of penguin counting – postmodern zoology. Postmodern zoologists challenge old-style assumptions, such as that there are animals in zoos, that nobody is interested in goats and that children would much rather play on their Playstations than visit a zoo. Empirical zoologists have responded to this challenge by counting animals, goats and Playstations.

Zygote

Ovum rendered imperfect.

Afterword

If you haven't had enough yet, and you'd like to know more, then visit a page on the *Butterflies and Wheels* website (which was established to fight fashionable nonsense, and from where the dictionary originates), where we explain what is going on in each entry. It's here:

http://www.butterfliesandwheels.com/fdexplained.php